THE
MOM'S
GUIDE
TO A
GOOD
DIVORCE

Cover and Interior design: 1106 Design

For information about this title or to order other books and/or electronic
media, contact the publisher: Life Journey Experiences
lifejourneyexperiences.com

gooddivorce.guide

Print:
ISBN-13: 978-0-9975613-0-2

LCCN (Paperback only): 2016907465

eBook:
978-0-9975613-1-9

THE
MOM'S
GUIDE
TO A
GOOD
DIVORCE

WHAT TO THINK THROUGH
WHEN CHILDREN ARE INVOLVED

SARAH ARMSTRONG

This book is dedicated

to my daughter, Grace,

who is my inspiration to be

the best Mom possible...

This is written by a girl

who never, ever thought she would get a divorce,

who ended up getting a divorce

and what she learned along the way...

PREFACE

Just for the record...I am not an advocate for divorce. In an ideal world, couples that get married would happily stay together for the long term. Unfortunately, this is not always the case...and these days it is more common than ever.

The purpose of this book is not to help you to decide to get a divorce. It is meant to be a practical guide once the decision has been made to make this change in your life.

My goal in writing this book is to help women who have children go through this change and make it through both the process and the post-divorce phase with a positive outcome for both you and your children.

The reason I decided to write this book is because over the past five years since I went through this major change in my life...I have been asked by many friends to give them advice on how to go through the process and come out happy on the other end. Somehow, the girl who never, ever thought she would get a divorce has become a poster child for a "good divorce."

Over the years, my friends encouraged me to capture my coaching points because they really need to be shared with other women who are going through divorce, so that is what I decided to do.

It is important to note that I am not a therapist or attorney... nor do I have a degree that would make me an expert on the topic of divorce.

I am someone who never actually expected to get divorced. I was raised Catholic by parents who have been happily married, in a true partnership, for almost 50 years. Always thought that would be the case for me as well, but sometimes things do not work out as you expect.

In sharing my thoughts, I also want to say that I am not looking to share details of why I got divorced.

However, I will share the decisions we made throughout our divorce as we always had our daughter, Grace, as the focus. We wanted to ensure that if we were going to go through this process (which would undoubtedly significantly impact her life given that she was only seven years old at the time) that we were doing all we could to keep her needs in mind throughout the entire process.

So...I decided to write this book as if I was sitting with one of my girlfriends in my living room talking through all of the details of divorce over a bottle of wine.

Each of my friends with whom I have spent time discussing their divorces had their own specific situations with unique dynamics that led to divorce. Throughout these discussions, it became clear that even though every situation is different... there are universal decisions we all have to make, regardless of our situations.

Based on these discussions, I tried to bring my friends' various experiences into the guidance provided in this book. The profiles of these women include...a CEO, a public relations executive, a marketing executive, a sales executive, an attorney and a CEO of the home (aka a stay-at-home mom).

From whichever perspective you are reading this book... either as a working mom or stay-at-home mom...some of the guidance provided is universal and, in some instances, there are different considerations that you have to think through during this process depending on your situation.

Throughout this book, there are points covered which are specific to a certain socio-economic situation. Please feel free to skip over these points if they are not relevant to you, however, the vast majority of the guidance in this book should be helpful as you navigate this journey.

From my standpoint, I was in the fortunate situation where I earned a comparable amount to my ex-husband. From a financial standpoint, I entered into the post-divorce stage able to support myself, my daughter and the lifestyle I wanted... which I realize is not necessarily the case for many women going through this process.

The irony in the fact that I have decided to write this book is that I have always said that I never wanted to be defined by my divorce. I am living an amazing life...raising a very special daughter...engaged in a rewarding career...with a supportive family and wonderful friends...and a special companion who I get to relax and have fun with...so I have chosen not to dwell on my divorce.

However, I felt compelled to share my experiences in the hope that this guidance builds your strength and confidence and helps you prepare for the discussions you need to have... and the decisions you need to make...always keeping your children as a priority, but also putting yourself as a priority.

If you have to go through this significant life change, hopefully at the end of the process and as you start to live your new life with your children...you can put it in the category of a "good divorce."

A GOOD DIVORCE

A year after my divorce was final...Grace and I were standing in line at CVS waiting to check out. There was a *People* magazine displayed at the counter that had Jennifer Lopez and Marc Antony on the cover and the headline said something about them getting a divorce. Grace pointed to the cover and said, "Mommy, is that a good divorce or a bad divorce?" I was caught off guard by her question, but I stopped and asked her, "Grace, I am not sure...how would you explain a good divorce and a bad divorce?" Grace shared that "a good divorce is when the mommy and daddy are nice to each other and try to be friends...like you and daddy and a bad divorce is when the mommy and daddy fight and scream at each other."

I walked out of the CVS that day and reflected on what Grace had just shared...as she was able to categorize our divorce as a "good divorce." I knew the approach her dad and I were taking to our divorce was working.

THE GUIDE

This is actually the guide which would have been helpful to refer to when I was going through my divorce from both an emotional and practical standpoint. So...I have structured "The Guide" in specific phases relating to the change you are about to make in your life. The reason this should be useful is that you can read a section at a time, absorb and process what you have read, then set the book aside if you need to... until you are ready to read the next section.

There is so much to think through when you are going through this change, and what I have found from discussing all of these details with my girlfriends going through it is that they generally could only process one phase at a time...and only when they were ready for the next phase would we take the next steps on the journey.

It is an understatement to say that this is a very emotional process...and your emotions will come into play in some phases more than others. Give yourself time to process each phase as you need to.

There are many reasons that trigger a divorce and the reasons are often emotionally driven. So, you need to do all you can to...stop...collect yourself...be smart...and approach the process in a very conscious way...trying to take as much emotion out of the process as possible in order to achieve the outcome that you desire.

My friend who was going through the process shared this quote…"Walk away from a marriage…don't run."

Another friend offered…"Calm is your friend" when going through a divorce. The calmer (and more level-headed) you can be when navigating the process, the better the outcome will be in the end.

It can be overwhelming to see all of the points that you need to think through during the process listed out. It is important to recognize this is a process, so take it in bite-sized pieces that you can handle…

BITE-SIZED PIECES

A small note about the design of this book...it has been outlined specifically for the mindset of a woman who is starting to think through what it will take to get divorced.

So...I have decided to put only one topic on a page and have included as much white space as possible to provide space for you to think about the specific topic.

Only turn the page when you are ready for the next topic... that could be tomorrow...next week...next month...

CONTENTS

PREPARING for the CHANGE

DURING the CHANGE

POST the CHANGE

REFLECTIONS...FIVE YEARS AFTER

PREPARING for the CHANGE

The Decision

The first thing I want to share is that the decision to get a divorce is one of the toughest decisions a person can make... especially when children are involved. The complexity of going through this major life change is much more significant than if a husband and wife who do not have children decide to part ways. When you have the lives of your children to consider, arriving at the decision to actually trigger a divorce has to be thought through very carefully...and is never a decision to be taken lightly.

One of the questions that always came up with each of my girlfriends as they were contemplating triggering their divorce was...

"How do I know I have done everything I can before making the decision to get a divorce?"

The follow-up point was...

"I want to be able to tell my children that I tried everything I could to make the marriage work before going down this path."

This was a key point I needed to address before I finally made my decision...that I could someday tell Grace with total confidence that I had done everything I could do to try to save our marriage.

It should be noted that there is no required timeframe for making this decision...it could take a week...a month...a year... or multiple years.

Among my girlfriends, I have observed a wide range of time-frames from contemplating getting a divorce to actually beginning the process. The important thing to remember is that you will know when it is the right time to make your decision.

One of my friends reflected on the irony of the two feelings most of us have relating to the person we chose to marry... "At one point in your life, you know he's the one...and then you end up realizing...he is not the one."

As I stated earlier, I am not an advocate for divorce...I think couples should try to do everything they can to keep their family together. However, there does come a point in a relationship where the two individuals are so unhappy that the only choice is to divorce.

Leading up to the decision, there are many paths to take... some paths involve going to therapy (individual therapy or couples therapy)...others talk to friends and family...some pursue a combination of the two.

My therapist (whom I went to for many years)...said to me during one of our sessions, "Sarah, you are sitting on an egg (aka my marriage)...and you do not want any cracks to show. When you are ready for the cracks to show, then you will be ready to get a divorce." She then told me that we had talked through every angle and exhausted all topics and to come back when I was ready to get a divorce...she basically fired me.

My therapist also told me that if I still had things to work through in my marriage, then I should work those through in advance of triggering a divorce. It is important to note that you do not want to work through your marriage issues during a divorce...that is not the intent of the process. It is essential to figure out if there is something worth saving in your marriage...and try to do everything you can to save it... before deciding to proceed with a divorce.

Sometimes the decision to get a divorce is not up to you...as your spouse has made the decision. Alternatively, you may be compelled to divorce if your spouse has issues that cannot be resolved...such as emotionally unavailable...inability to be faithful...bipolar disorder... anger management issues...or addiction (such as alcohol, drugs, gambling, sex). Whatever the catalyst that brings you to the point where you are getting a divorce, making the final decision to do so...especially when children are involved...is incredibly difficult.

Once the decision is made to get a divorce, then the focus should be on making it through the process, and the post-divorce era with minimal drama, and as few emotional scars as possible for everyone involved... you, your children and your soon-to-be ex-husband.

So...whatever brought you to this point, which has most likely been a roller-coaster of emotions...whether it has been your decision, a joint decision, or your spouse's decision...regardless, you are now at the point where we need to help you prepare to think through the things you need to think through...

Where to Start

Once the decision has been made that there is no other option but to move forward with a divorce...it can be overwhelming to think about where to even start the process.

Once I made the decision, I also made a clear decision about how I wanted to go through the process.

Basically, going through a divorce is similar to managing a project...so, I have broken down the key decisions to think through... and you can work through these decisions in each phase. Please know that these points do not need to be addressed in the order I have outlined, but this is the order that I followed making this change.

Mindset is Essential

It is important to recognize that this is an incredibly emotional time in your life, so what is required when a divorce is triggered is a calm, level-headed and practical mindset for going through the process.

This may be a very tall order given the dynamics of what has led you to divorce, but if you want to try to manage one of the most difficult events in your life and help your children through it as well, then approaching each decision with a mindset of positive intent is essential.

Ensure you give yourself the time to work through the details of each decision...as there are many. At times, you will need to put aside your emotions until you have worked through the details...or there may be times when you need to put away the details until you have worked through your emotions. At the end of the process, you want to ensure you made the right decisions for you and your children.

Understand Your Finances

I cannot stress enough how important it is for you to understand your finances. For some couples, where the wife has always handled the finances, this is an easier step. If you are like I was, and your husband had been managing the finances during your marriage...it is time to get educated and informed on where everything stands from a financial standpoint.

If you do not understand your finances or how to think through the planning required, then either hire a financial planner or find a friend that is financially savvy and ask them for help. This is what I did...and it was an important step in helping me understand the financial picture I was dealing with...and what I needed to think through from a financial standpoint moving forward.

I had actually been very removed from the day-to-day of our finances. When I decided to engage and start to understand where things stood with our finances...I realized that I had a lot to learn.

This can seem like a daunting task...especially if you have completely deferred the task to your husband, but you need to take the first steps to understanding all of the details of all of your accounts...household bills, credit card accounts, checking accounts, savings accounts, investment accounts, retirement accounts, children's 529 accounts, taxes (property and income), car loans, mortgage, umbrella insurance policies, health insurance, life insurance, disability insurance, real estate investments, foreign bank accounts, debt, etc. The list can be long, and the challenge is to ensure you are clear on all of the accounts that exist (including whose name is on each account and the account number).

If this sounds overwhelming, just take it one step at a time. The good news is that the work you do to understand your current financial picture will help you down the road when you need to manage these financial details for yourself in the next phase of your life. Think of this as an empowering step, rather than an intimidating one.

Also, once the process is kicked off, it may not be feasible to withdraw or transfer funds from the accounts you share with your husband, so make sure you are clear on what transactions are (or are not) allowed from these accounts during the process.

If you are in a situation where you do not think you have full visibility of your financial situation (and you do not believe your husband is going to be transparent on these details), then you may need to hire a forensic accountant to help ensure you have the clearest possible picture of your financial situation before triggering your divorce. It should be noted that attorneys are generally not qualified to be forensic accountants.

My recommendation is to fully understand your current financial picture well in advance of triggering the process. The financial game changes once you and your husband start down the path to divorce...and it is essential to clearly understand the picture before heading down this path.

As you enter into your divorce discussions, you will need to be able to clearly outline what you believe it takes financially to support your life and your children's lives...from the present and until they are 21...when they will hopefully be on the path to supporting themselves.

Prepare Your Budget

To start, outline a detailed household budget. This should include all the expenses it takes to run your life and your children's lives.

Next, outline the key expenses you see over the next one, three, and five years...whether it is a home maintenance project, trips you are planning to take with your children, buying a new car, your share of your children's tuition for private school or college, etc.

If possible, you should try to have at least three months of expenses in the bank as savings...as you may need to draw on these savings as you are going through the transition post-divorce.

Determine Approach to Divorce

When we decided to get a divorce, I explored the different approaches...and there are definitely different established options these days to consider...specifically, the Traditional Divorce and Collaborative Divorce. Each approach has considerations you need to think through to determine which approach would be best for your situation.

Traditional Divorce

The Traditional Divorce approach is when each person gets an attorney (or you use the same attorney) and you work through every detail with your attorneys. This is how many couples approach divorce...and I have watched many friends go through this Traditional approach.

It is important to note that the Traditional approach can be used for the most straightforward and the most complicated situations.

Collaborative Divorce

I had heard about the Collaborative Divorce process and researched whether or not this approach could work for us. The reason this is so unique is that it is a team-based approach that requires each person to have a coach and an attorney. In addition, the couple is also supported by a financial neutral advisor and a child specialist. The financial neutral advisor is neutral to the couple and has full visibility of all financial details and will advise on how to split up all of the assets between you and your ex-husband. The child specialist meets with the parents and the children (during separate sessions) to help think through decisions which are being made relating to the children.

This group of six specialists works closely together to help the couple finalize all details relating to the divorce. This group also works to ensure that throughout the process both parents keep the children as the main focus in decision-making.

By the way, it may sound like an expensive approach, however, it can actually be a more efficient way (both in terms of time and money) than the Traditional approach.

I truly believe that part of the reason Grace could refer to our divorce as "a good divorce" is due to the Collaborative approach. I would encourage you to consider speaking with an attorney who specializes in the Collaborative approach in your area to determine if your situation meets the criteria for a Collaborative Divorce.

Traditional vs. Collaborative Divorce

The one point that can help you determine if you want to proceed with a Traditional versus a Collaborative approach is whether you and your spouse can interact in an amicable way to talk through all of the details required during the process. This means you and your husband need to be able to discuss various points...both with coaches in the room and without coaches in the room. There is a strong requirement (and expectation) within the Collaborative approach that the two of you can have productive discussions about specific topics in order to come to the best possible agreement for the two of you and your children. If this is feasible, then a Collaborative approach may be the path you want to explore.

If you are in a scenario where it would not be feasible to have a discussion with your ex-husband, then you may need to consider the Traditional approach.

Determining whether to use the Traditional or Collaborative approach is a personal decision. Either way, you will end up getting through the process...and whichever you decide to use...the points I am going to share with you can apply to either approach.

Find the Best Legal Support for You

The decision to call an attorney and engage in a discussion about potentially getting a divorce can seem like a big deal. Just remember that having a discussion with an attorney does not necessarily commit you to going down the path of getting a divorce.

When you take this step, the initial discussion with an attorney should help you understand what you need to think through if you decide to go down this path...and there is nothing wrong with understanding your rights as you are making your decision.

Meeting with an attorney may also help you determine what kind of process is preferred for your specific situation... Traditional vs. Collaborative...and the appropriate style of attorney that will best fit your situation.

Whether you decide to go through the Traditional or Collaborative approach, you will still need to confirm who you want to engage from a legal standpoint to support you throughout the process.

If you are going to use the Traditional approach, then the best advice I can provide is to ask your friends who have gone through a Traditional divorce to recommend potential attorneys.

If you are going to use the Collaborative Approach, then there will be a list of attorneys online who are qualified to work within the Collaborative process within your area.

If you have a list of attorneys you are considering (for either approach), then you should take the opportunity to interview each attorney to see who would best fit your situation...as you want an attorney you can trust, who will listen to you and understand the role you want them to play in your discussions.

If the recommendations you have received are not directly from a friend, then you should also ask for referrals.

It is important for you to decide the type of attorney that you want to engage as there is a wide spectrum of options when it comes to divorce attorneys. There are different types of attorneys to handle different types of divorces...some are hard-nosed pit bulls and others are collaborative peacemakers...both serve a purpose. Depending on your situation, you will need determine the type of attorney that best suits your needs.

Based on initial discussions, if the attorney does not represent how you want the process to be handled, then look for a different option. It is important that you are represented in a way that reflects the tone you want to take for your divorce.

There will usually be a charge for the initial consultation, so ensure you do your homework up front, and get to a short list of attorneys that you would want to "interview", so you can minimize the cost of this stage in the process.

It is key to set aside some money in case you want to engage an attorney for an initial consultation before your husband knows what you are considering...the amount you will need to set aside will depend on the attorney, but a safe amount would be $500 - $1,000.

Once you get further along in your legal discussions, you will need to determine who will be paying attorney's fees throughout the process.

Try to be as efficient as possible when working with your attorney...as they charge by the hour for both providing guidance, and for listening. They are more than willing to think through everything with you, but you need to come in prepared to discuss the details you want to cover with them. Don't confuse your attorney with your therapist...it can be an expensive mistake.

From my standpoint, I was looking for an attorney who would guide me through the process without any drama, was straightforward in their approach, and would move through the process quickly.

The decision in terms of which attorney to engage is a very important decision that will have a significant impact on the process.

Define Your Ideal Timeframe

The topic of timeframe is a difficult one to discuss in terms of specifics as each situation is completely different. An "ideal" timeframe can be a challenge to define, depending on the various elements of your divorce and how much you need to work through to gain final alignment with your spouse.

Over the years, I have been on journeys with my girlfriends that have taken six months from decision to final divorce, and other friends where the time from initial discussion until finalization was over ten years. One girlfriend used the expression, "There are no wrong answers" in terms of the timing of this decision...it is unique to each situation.

However, try to define with your lawyer the "ideal" timeframe for the full process. There are factors that could impact this timing such as whether your soon-to-be ex-husband is ready to work through the various details required in the process or he might have a different "ideal" timeframe in mind. Also, in certain instances, my girlfriends did not realize that they needed to push their attorneys to move through the process...to basically keep their divorce "top of mind" with their attorney.

A girlfriend who went through a prolonged process shared this perspective, "If you miss your goal, or are not able to control the process, then do not be too hard on yourself or get deflated. After all, it is an incredibly unique and humanizing process to experience, so learn about yourself. Everyone gets through it eventually."

So...define your ideal timeframe, then make it very clear to your spouse and your attorney the timeframe you believe it should take to go through the process. Also, if you have defined a timeframe, then you need to take a proactive role in driving decisions to meet the timeframe. If you have done your preparation in advance (which is discussed throughout this phase), then the process will be quicker from start to finish.

When I finally made the decision to make the initial call to my attorney for an interview, I was clear on the timeframe for how I wanted to handle my divorce. My attorney listened, then provided feedback that the timeframe that I was planning on was aggressive, but achievable... if we hit specific deadlines along the way.

When we completed the divorce within the timeframe I had initially outlined, my attorney called me and said, "You were not kidding about moving through this process quickly." I just smiled...it had taken six months from start to finish...which was the timeframe we had outlined during our initial discussion.

Define What You Want Your Life to Look Like

When deciding to make this major change in your life, one of the most important things to think about is how you envision your life (and your children's lives) after you are divorced. There are many aspects to your life post the change... some you will need to think through in advance... others you will not be able to really start thinking about until you are through the process.

However, it is important to realize that you may not have the same lifestyle you had when you were married...as the change could impact...where you live, where your children go to school, the car you drive, the travel you can afford, and many other considerations. A good starting point for this thought process is to begin by thinking through the trade-offs...

Think through Trade-offs

There is always compromise at different points in a marriage...and this is one of those instances where you really need to think through the compromises that you are willing to make...as there are going to be trade-offs that come with being divorced.

The important thing is for you to get clear on what you are willing to trade off...what you want to fight for...and the things that do not matter to you at all. The clarity you have on these points will have implications on your life and your children's lives.

So...take some time to think about the things that are genuinely important to you...the things that you want to control... and what you are willing to let go...this is where you pick your battles (in advance)...then, let the rest go...

It is important not to show your hand...as you can use those points that are unimportant to you as leverage for other things that are important to you.

As you head into discussions with your spouse, there will be surprises and disappointments...moments when you think to yourself..."I thought I knew this person"...so, you need to prepare yourself and arm yourself with emotional toughness to get through these discussions.

This is a defining part of the process...as this will set the tone for the divorce, and for the relationship you will have with your ex-husband post-divorce.

Confirm Where You Want to Live

One of the first major decisions is where you are going to live after the divorce. The challenge with this point is there are a lot of variables in terms of the details of this decision. If you have the option of staying in the house where you have been raising your children...based on what I have observed, this is the best option...at least for the first year (or two) after a divorce is final.

There are so many adjustments that you and your children go through during the first year of a divorce that if you can minimize the need for your children to adjust to two new homes all at once...that is ideal. The children will already have to adjust to at least one new home when they go and live with their father for the days they are with him.

However, keeping the house that you have been living in may not be an option. If your home is connected to bad memories or traumatic situations, a fresh start may be best for you and your children. If this is the case, then finding a place that you can create as your new home is a key point to think through.

If your children are in public school, then there is also the consideration of continuing to live in the same school district, so there is no need to change schools due to moving homes.

If you need to find a new place to live, then think how you want to position to your children the fact that you are going to be moving...and frame it up in a way that shows your children that you will be creating a positive, happy home together with them.

How to Tell Your Children

The approach you take to telling your children you are getting a divorce is a very important step in the process. Ideally, you would tell your children together (with their father) at a point when you could explain to them that you have decided to get a divorce...and you feel confident answering a number of the questions that they will naturally ask at this point. For example, "Where are we going to live?"..."Where is Dad going to live?"..."How often will we see Dad?"...and the list goes on.

The important point to remember is that most children are going to focus on questions that revolve around them...and what this change will mean in their lives...specifically from a "logistics of life" standpoint. If you can put yourself in their shoes and anticipate the questions that will come from them... the better prepared you will be for this discussion. This will be a conversation they will remember for the rest of their lives...guaranteed.

When we were done telling Grace the news, she asked one or two logistics questions, then said, "Can I go play now?" Again, this is partly due to the fact that she was seven years old...and partly because this is how children generally process this information at a young age.

If you are telling children who are older, there may be additional questions that they will ask, depending upon how aware they are of the dynamics between you and your husband leading up to the decision to get a divorce.

If the two of you can address your children's questions as a united front during this initial discussion, this will set the tone for future discussions with your children during and after the divorce.

There is also the consideration of whether to tell your children together or separately. My friends have used both approaches (and in each instance they have worked well), so this really depends on how you think your children will process this news.

If your children are unaware of any difficulties in your marriage...as you and your husband have not been giving signals that anything is wrong...then the less information you share, the better...until they ask specific questions, and you decide how to answer them.

Similar to adults, children need to process the divorce one step at a time...so, offering up more information than they are asking for at the time is not recommended. There will be other questions, but they need to process what is happening, and will ask their questions throughout the process. Once they are aware of the change that will be taking place in their lives, it is important to give them the space and time they need to process this news in their own way.

When & Where to Tell Your Children

There are all types of scenarios in terms of how this could unfold...

In an ideal situation, you will have worked through as many details as possible before you tell your children...because then you will be well-prepared to answer all of their questions. If you can strive to achieve this, then you can protect your children. The consequences of divorce are difficult enough... your children should not have to live through every detail of the process.

Depending on the ages of your children, you may be able to get through certain phases of your divorce before you have to tell them. If you have older children, you will probably need to tell them sooner rather than later because they will most likely be aware that something is going on.

When you have multiple children at different ages, they can react very differently...and you may want to think through specific approaches for each child. It could be helpful to engage a family therapist to help your children as they process this decision.

If you have the opportunity to choose an ideal time to tell your children, it is recommended to avoid holidays and birthdays. The ideal timing will be based on knowing your children and what makes the most sense for them.

It is recommended to tell children in a familiar place, where they feel comfortable and secure in the surroundings.

In one instance, my friend decided to tell her children on their family vacation...because it allowed her daughters to process the news before going back to their day-to-day lives. Another friend told her children two weeks before school started... to allow her children to adjust to the news before going back to school. In both of these instances, my friends felt the approach they used for telling their children worked well.

It is also important to think through telling those individuals who are around your children...teachers, nannies, friends, neighbors, coaches, etc. These individuals may be the first people to whom your children mention the news. When you provide them a heads-up, you may want to give them talking points for how you would like this to be explained to your children, so they can appropriately respond if your children mention this news to them.

One friend shared...when telling these individuals the news, be clear that you do not want them prompting your children on the subject. It should be up to your children to raise it with them, when (and if) they feel comfortable.

What to Tell Your Children

It is essential to think through what you will tell your children are the reasons for the divorce.

Depending on what triggered the divorce and how openly the triggers have been discussed within your home, may define how you approach this discussion with your children.

This is one of those points that will be unique to your situation...we just need to remember that our children are very impressionable (regardless of their age)...so what they are told about either parent...will stay with them for a very long time.

In discussing this point with my friends, some consistent guidance was "Less is more"..."Keep it simple"... "Do not overshare"...

Just remember the points you do share need to be thought through carefully.

The best divorces I have witnessed have been situations where...regardless of the reasons...the children are unaware of why their parents got divorced...and the parents have made a conscious effort to protect their children from fully understanding the situation.

Someday the children may gain a full understanding of the situation that triggered their parent's divorce, but hopefully it will be at an age when they can process this information appropriately.

Be Clear & Consistent on Your Messaging with Family & Friends

One of the key points discussed during the Collaborative approach is to be clear on the messaging you will use with family and friends regarding why you decided to get a divorce. Also, be clear if you are providing background that should not be shared with your children.

It is important to stay consistent with the messaging you are communicating and not to change the messaging just because you are having a bad day.

The messaging does not need to be extensive...it just needs to be consistent.

People will be interested in the details, but whatever you share reflects on you as well as your children. Just remember that your soon-to-be ex-husband is and always will be your children's father.

Messaging for Family

Depending on your situation, telling your family that you are getting a divorce may be a straightforward discussion (if the decision is not coming as a surprise to them)...or it could be a very intense scenario where you need to provide the background and context. In either scenario, ensure you take the time to have the discussions with your family (ideally in person), so they can be there for you as you embark on the process.

Although in certain instances it may be a challenging dynamic, ideally, your family should try to follow your lead and attempt to keep emotions out of it, stay focused on the children...and support you and the children throughout the process.

Messaging for Friends

Think about the approach you want to take to tell your friends that you are getting a divorce. First, in terms of who you want to ensure hears the news directly from you...and, also when and how you tell your friends. It is never a quick conversation, and if it is a surprise...which it was in my case...it takes time to provide background and context as to why you are making this change in your life.

Also, before triggering my divorce, I prioritized my friendships with my girlfriends...ensuring that I had a strong support system in place...because I knew I would need these friendships more than ever.

For your outer circle of friends, define a well thought-through, concise message. The goal is to avoid making your divorce the latest bit of gossip around town.

It is also important to think about who you do not need in your midst during the process...basically, anyone who is not supportive of the decision you have made to make the change. Assess your energy takers versus energy givers...during this process, you need to be around those that give you energy and support.

Therapy for You

Based on my personal experience, I am an advocate of individual therapy. It is definitely worthwhile to find the right therapist...one who is able to help you think through the things you need to think through...listen when you need them to listen...and push you a bit when you need a little nudge. If you have established a relationship with a therapist, then they can be there for you during and after the divorce...as needed.

One of my girlfriends shared..."My therapy sessions are like 'a spa for my mind' because I get a chance to open up, exhale and detox emotionally."

Therapy for Your Children

I am also an advocate of children going to therapy in the very early days of learning that their parents are getting a divorce. As I mentioned, the Collaborative approach actually requires children to go to a child specialist, who focuses on children of divorce. We were fortunate to find a child specialist who was able to see Grace right after we told her about the divorce, and for the following six months.

The reason I found this to be such an important step in our journey is that, from the very beginning, Grace was able to express her opinion to someone who understood what she was going through. In addition, Grace was able to ask questions during her counseling sessions that she was not able to ask either of us. She was also able to have someone who could coach her about what she was about to experience...and share some tips with her about how to handle this new reality.

Prepare for Transition...
Stay-at-Home vs. Working Mom

As I stated in the beginning, I have always been a working mom and I am grateful for that being the case...as it has given me more flexibility in some of the decisions I needed to make during the process. I am also fortunate because I enjoy what I do each day...which is so important in life.

Based on discussions with many friends who are going through divorces...some of whom are stay-at-home moms and others who are working moms...there are some points that all moms need to think about when going through the process.

As you would expect, there are specific points relevant to just working moms, or to just stay-at-home moms. These points have been outlined in separate sections, so you can read the section that is relevant to your situation.

Stay-at-Home Mom...
Striving For Self-Sufficiency

I have never been a stay-at-home mom, but I have many close friends who have chosen to stay home and raise their children...which I truly believe is one of the hardest jobs in the world. I know that I am not capable of staying home, so all of my comments come with the greatest respect for those who do...

The challenge when you go through a divorce as a stay-at-home mom is to figure out which aspects of your life will continue as they have been during your marriage and which will evolve due to the change in dynamics. As I have watched my friends go through this...it has been both difficult and rewarding to see the decisions they have to make to put themselves on a path to being self-sufficient...as a big challenge in being a stay-at-home mom is the post-divorce dependence on alimony and child support.

If you are a stay-at-home mom, then it will be important to determine if/when you will need to start thinking about working to support yourself and your family. Based on what I have observed from my friends who are stay-at-home moms, they have all taken some time post-divorce to regroup, before figuring out what they want to do from a career standpoint.

However, there is a point when a stay-at-home mom may decide she wants to work to support herself and her children. From what I have observed of my friends working through this decision, it does take time to determine the best career path to explore. So, I would not wait too long after the divorce to start thinking about what you would want to do from a career standpoint...as you want to give yourself time to find the right role...and not just take any job because you are under pressure to make money.

One friend who is a stay-at-home mom mentioned that she received counsel from her attorney to not start a job before the divorce is final and alimony has been agreed to in the final settlement. If you do go back to work before the divorce is final, then this could impact the final financial settlement.

Another friend who is a stay-at-home mom shared, "It may feel like a scary thing to re-enter the work force, but try to look at it as another opportunity for growth and independence."

Working Mom...
Striving for Balance

If you are already a working mom...then you potentially have more flexibility in many of the topics that have been covered so far, such as what to do with the house and childcare, but the one thing you can't do is be in two places at the same time.

My one bit of advice for working moms is to start to live the balance you think you will need to live leading up to and through divorce...do not wait until you are officially divorced. The reason this is important is that there is conditioning that needs to take place...for you, for your children, and for your workplace...in terms of how you will be operating as you move forward. It is important to take into account the fact that you will not have another parent at home for backup on a day-to-day basis.

It is actually no different than when you had your first child... my counsel to first-time moms is to start living your "working mom" schedule while you are pregnant...so you condition yourself to manage the various aspects of your life. Going through a divorce can be a similar adjustment to having your first child. It is a significant life event which requires you to reflect on all aspects of your life...and think through the changes that will be required on a day-to-day basis.

One important point is to ensure you bring your boss and potentially a small group of colleagues into the loop as soon as you can...as you cannot underestimate the time entailed in going through each step of the divorce process. There will be times you will need to be out of the office for various meetings required for the process.

However, keep the circle small in terms of those individuals at work who know that you are going through a divorce...as your personal life does not need to contribute to the hallway chatter.

Also, consider how much travel you are able and willing to do, given your new arrangement from a custody standpoint... and, the timeframe of your business travel. There are also potentially certain nights you will not able to go to a business dinner because there will be nights you have your children. These dynamics need to be managed to ensure you can deliver on what you need to do from a career standpoint, while also spending the time you need to with your children...especially as you are transitioning into this new way of living as a family.

We need to recognize that it is an on-going challenge to strive for balance in the various aspects of our lives. The definition of what "balance" looks like is different for each working mom.

Just try to be realistic as you work to balance the needs of your family and your career when you go through your divorce. It takes time to figure out the day-to-day juggling act of being a single working mom...and what will work best for you and your children.

Build Your Support Network

As you are starting to think through the changes you are about to go through...it is important to build a support network of friends and family who can help you along the way. There are a wide range of things you need to think about, so seek out those who have gone through (or are going through) the same thing. They will be helpful sounding boards as you think about the details involved in navigating the process.

This support network is also an important group to have around you both before, during and after the divorce.

A word of caution...I would recommend keeping the circle of friends who know all of the details to a very small crew. It can be exhausting to educate your circle with every new development of where things stand throughout the process, so you should be very conscious of who you bring into this inner circle.

It is also important to keep in mind to only share details with those friends that can keep those details to themselves... especially if there are details you are trying to protect your children from knowing about the divorce. If you have not yet told your children that you are getting a divorce...you definitely want to avoid them hearing it from someone else...before you have had a chance to tell them. We have all heard friends say, "...but I only told one person."

DURING the CHANGE

Outline Parenting Plan Together

Whether or not you use Collaborative or Traditional approach to divorce, you should work with your spouse to outline a Parenting Plan which outlines how you will jointly manage your children's lives. This is helpful because it becomes the point of reference if there is ever a debate or disagreement relating to decisions you have made about your children during the divorce process.

I will go through each of the topics in the Parenting Plan and share my perspective on how we thought through the details related to each topic. There could be additional details included in the Parenting Plan that you will discuss during your divorce process, but the points I will cover should help you think through the most important components of the Parenting Plan you want to cover with your soon-to-be ex-husband.

A couple of important points as you start to think through your Parenting Plan...

Try to ensure you have full clarity on each point. There may be points you and your spouse want to stay "flexible" on...which may seem okay at the time...but it is better to try to align on all of the specific points and have them documented in the Parenting Plan. If you want to be flexible down the road, then you can make this decision. However, if you are not clear up front, it is sometimes tough to agree on these points that were left as "flexible" after you are divorced...especially if "other perspectives" are introduced into the discussion.

Also, try to refrain from asking your children to weigh in on the decisions outlined in the Parenting Plan or put them in the middle of points that may be debated as you finalize specific points...your children should never have to take sides.

Custody

There are two types of custody you need to think through... Legal Custody and Physical Custody. This is one of the most important decisions you will make regarding your divorce... because it will set the tone for all of the other decisions that will be discussed within the Parenting Plan.

To start, you need to decide if you want primary Legal Custody and Physical Custody, whether you want your ex-husband to have primary custody for either of these aspects, or if you want to share custody and have joint Legal Custody and/or joint Physical Custody.

This is a topic that you will need to discuss in detail with your attorney to ensure you understand the details relating to each option.

Legal Custody

Legal Custody is a type of child custody that grants a parent the right to make important, long-term decisions regarding their children. This may include decisions relating to education, medical/dental care, religious upbringing and finances.

There is also Joint Legal Custody where each parent is granted equal rights with regards to decision-making for the children. This can be an ideal arrangement for situations where the parents can communicate with each other and make decisions together regarding their children.

Physical Custody

Physical Custody (primary) is a term that is often used to denote the parent with whom the children live the majority of the time.

Joint Physical Custody means that each parent shares time with the children, but not necessarily equal time. However, there is an option within joint custody where the children have a primary physical residence with one parent.

Decision-Making

In terms of decision-making for your children...there are the day-to-day decisions (such as what you feed your children for meals) that need to be made, and then there are the major decisions (such as the type of school you want your children to attend). It is important to be clear on how you want to handle each of these types of decisions with your ex-husband...as these decisions can become challenging in terms of your interactions with your ex-husband, if they are not clearly defined prior to finalizing the divorce.

Day-to-Day Decisions

Each parent will make day-to-day decisions regarding childcare when the children are with them.

However, if there was a decision that impacted the other parent's time with the children...for example, an invitation for a sleepover that fell on the weekend the other parent had the children...then this would be a decision where the other parent should be weighing in.

Major Decisions

If there are any major decisions relating to the children, then the parents should discuss these together. There are four categories that are important to be very clear on...healthcare (non-emergency), education, religion and extracurricular activities. It is essential to clearly define which parent will have final decision rights for each of these categories and when decisions must be made jointly.

Healthcare

If your child has a serious injury or illness (at either household), the expectation should be set that each of you will inform the other within a specific time period. If the child requires non-emergency surgery, then the other parent should be consulted (if time permits). Also, if your child ever needs elective surgery, then decide in advance if both parents will weigh into this decision.

Education

This would include decisions relating to where your children will go to school, tuition, tutoring, college decisions, music or other educational activities your children might be involved in over the years.

Religion

This could include decisions relating to what religion the child follows...or which church, synagogue or temple to attend... and whether the child attends religious education classes.

Extracurricular Activities

This would include all decisions relating to what your children are participating in outside of school hours.

Parenting Approach

There are other decisions relating to the parenting approach with your children that you may want to think through and discuss with your ex-husband as part of your Parenting Plan. For example, the approach you will take to disciplining your children if they misbehave...or the bedtime you would like to target for your children...or the principles around cell phone or computer usage at your respective homes. There are a wide range of points to think through relating to your parenting approach. If you can define and align these points up front, it can help to maintain a consistent approach to parenting your children in both homes.

Resolving Conflicts

It is helpful to think through in advance how you want to address any major conflicts that may arise with your ex-husband post-divorce when there are strong disagreements on major decisions. Even in an amicable divorce, conflicts are going to happen, so you need to think through how you want to approach these situations.

Within the Collaborative Divorce process, there are specific steps that are agreed to in terms of resolving conflict which entail engaging a third party to help facilitate the discussion.

There is also a consideration regarding steps you will want to take in advance of any further legal action, if you come to a point where you cannot agree with your ex-husband on a specific major decision. This may entail counseling, coaching, mediation (by a neutral party chosen by both parents) or arbitration. If none of these approaches work to resolve the conflict, then it will require you to go to court to have a judge help to resolve the conflict.

My girlfriend had significant conflict in her divorce. Based on her experience, she recommends finding a coach who specializes in conflict resolution. This will enable you to take the disagreement out of the hands of the attorneys and work with a specialist who can help the two of you resolve this conflict with as little drama as possible.

Scheduling

If joint custody is the approach you are taking...then there are a wide range of scheduling options to consider including 5-2-2-5...week-on/week-off...nesting...or flexible scheduling.

5-2-2-5

The 5-2-2-5 approach is where one parent has the children for five days in a given week, and the other parent has the children for two days...it then switches for the next week.

The schedule could look like this...

Mother – Friday / Saturday / Sunday / Monday / Tuesday

Father – Wednesday / Thursday / Friday / Saturday / Sunday

This essentially means that the children are with one parent for Monday/Tuesday nights, and the other parent for Wednesday/ Thursday nights...and then each parent alternates weekends.

We have had a positive experience using the 5-2-2-5 approach. It is worth noting that we have tried to stay as consistent as possible with Grace's schedule. However, given both of our travel demands, there are weeks when we have had to adjust our schedules.

There are some nuances that we have defined within this approach. For example, Grace comes home each day to my house...and my ex-husband picks her up from my house at 6pm on the nights he will have her for the night. This has allowed Grace to have consistency in coming to one place each day after school.

Also, it is helpful to define if there will be any changes to the schedule during the summer, when your children are out of school. We have kept our 5-2-2-5 schedule the same during the summer, in terms of where Grace will sleep each night.

Week-on/Week-off

The week-on/week-off approach is also an option...although the major consideration with this approach is missing an entire week with your children...and an entire school week... which can be difficult...especially depending on the ages of the children.

There are multiple ways you could structure the week on/ week off schedule. Some of my friends have set the schedule to go from Sunday to Sunday and others have decided to go from Wednesday to Wednesday, so each parent gets to be a part of the school week.

Nesting

Nesting is where the parents are the ones who move each week...and the kids stay in one house. There are definitely pros and cons to this approach. On the positive side, the children do not have to "travel" each week between homes. On the negative side, the parents are still "sharing" space... even if you are not there at the same time. Personally, I am not an advocate of using this approach. However, I have seen friends who have successfully used Nesting (generally for the first year or two after the divorce) to help their kids adjust to this major change in their lives.

Flexible

There is also the option of staying "flexible" with the schedule.

The only guidance I can provide is that enabling your children to know what days they are going to be at your place, versus your ex-husband's place, enables them to plan for where they are going to be…and can help them to settle into some type of routine in this new way of life. Also, if you do not put a defined schedule in place, then you will be continually discussing scheduling logistics with your ex-husband…which is not ideal and could lead to conflict.

Living in Different States

If you find yourself in a situation where one of you is going to be living in a different state (or country), there are specific considerations you will need to think through. Generally, there will be specific provisions within your agreement which outline the "rules" relating to the distance between the two parents... and in turn different scheduling options to consider. There are too many options to go into detail about, but it is worth highlighting that given the distance, there are usually unique scenarios you can consider (especially for summer vacations).

One of my girlfriends had the situation where she agreed that her daughter would spend six weeks in the summer with her ex-husband, since she did not see him as much during the school year. Her perspective was interesting...because at first she was reluctant to give up six weeks of summer with her daughter. However, it has turned out to be a good thing for everyone. Her daughter loves all the quality time with her dad and his new family, he gets to spend more time with her and take long vacations, and my girlfriend has six weeks every year where she can take a breath from being a full-time mom and having a full-time career. My girlfriend's six-week "mommy hiatus" has allowed her to tackle all the projects, activities and travel that she never seems to get to during the year when she is engaged in the experience of being a single working mom.

Define Best Scheduling Option Based on Your Situation

There are other scheduling arrangements that can be explored, and I have watched friends put various scenarios in place, so you will need to define the arrangement that works best for your specific situation.

If one parent will have primary custody, then generally the parent without primary custody gets one or two nights per week plus every other weekend.

If the distance between the parents' homes is too far away for weeknight visits, then there is the possibility of scheduling every other weekend visits for the children with the parent who does not have primary custody. In this situation, the children could potentially spend more time during summer break with this parent to make up for the time they did not get to see the children during the school year.

In addition to the specific schedule (in terms of the days of the week), it is helpful to agree on a transition time each day (e.g., drop-off/pick-up from school or house)...as well as who is responsible for dropping off and picking up the children.

Also, if one parent needs coverage for the children, the agreement should be that the other parent gets "first right of refusal" before anyone else is asked if they will watch your children.

If there is a need to change the schedule (and you are not able to agree on this change with your ex-husband), then you will need to decide whether it requires counseling, mediation or filing a modification with the Court.

Holidays & Summer Vacations

There are many holidays throughout the year that need to be considered from a scheduling standpoint. We have found it helpful to agree on an alternating annual schedule of who will take each holiday using even/odd numbered years as the approach. This means we alternate having Grace for a given holiday every other year.

It is beneficial to define the specific start and end time of each holiday...as this is helpful when parents are scheduling travel around a specific holiday.

Remember to think through travel time needed during holidays. It is not ideal to leave early in the morning or late at night to meet a schedule, so try to build in a day for transition which allows for flexibility.

If you will all be in the same city for the holiday, then you can agree for each parent to celebrate half the day with the children, or you could celebrate together if amicable.

Also, it is good to remember to include parents' and siblings' birthdays in this list of holidays, so you are clear on how you want to handle each of these special occasions.

There is an opportunity to clearly define how you want to handle summer vacations in terms of how many weeks either parent can have the children. For example, we can each take Grace for a two-week vacation during the summer. I have first choice of vacation dates each year, then my ex-husband can schedule his vacation dates.

Due to holiday weekends, there are times when the schedule becomes uneven...and one parent may have two weekends in a row. When this occurs, we have agreed to adjust the weekends to try to resume a "normal" schedule.

Holidays are Never Easy...
Even in a Good Divorce

Depending on how you decide to structure your divorce agreement, this may or may not be a consideration. In our case, we split the holidays...so one year I have Grace for Thanksgiving Day, but not for Christmas Day (and spend the second half of Christmas break with her)...the next year it switches.

I have to admit that the only part of being divorced that I have not gotten used to in the past five years is not being with Grace on those holidays that she spends with her father. It is not an easy time...and given my experience over the past five years...I have decided to travel during the holidays that I do not have Grace. Thankfully, I have a special companion in my life that I can travel with who is a fabulous diversion for me during these difficult holiday times. So, if you can...I would definitely recommend finding your diversion.

Transportation Arrangements

In terms of transitioning between homes, you need to agree on where these transitions should take place.

For example, we agreed that my ex-husband would pick-up and drop off Grace at my home.

However, we also added that I would drive Grace to school each morning, so the mornings she is staying at her dad's house, I pick her up there and take her to school. I like this arrangement, as this ensures that I have some quality time (20 minutes) each morning with Grace.

This does mean that we have not been involved in school carpools in the morning, but I definitely think the trade-off is worth it...as our time in the car is spent talking about a wide range of topics and listening to Grace's favorite music on our way to school.

There are other considerations that come into the day-to-day transitions between households.

It is helpful for each parent to be diligent in ensuring the children (and any required belongings) are ready when the other parent arrives to pick them up.

Each parent should try to make every effort to be on time in picking up the children at the defined time. We generally give each other 15 minutes of leeway during pick-ups and drop-offs (except, of course for school or other scheduled appointments).

Children Flying Alone

If you and your ex-husband are living in different states, then a key point to consider is whether or not you are comfortable with your children flying alone. My girlfriend's divorce agreement stipulated that both parents have to agree that the children can fly alone. One parent may be more comfortable with this concept than the other...and it is important for both of you to be comfortable with this decision.

This need for alignment does not only apply to parental visits...as it could apply to visiting grandparents or going to summer camp.

Communication

It is essential that each parent can communicate with the children as necessary...whether that means calling after school to see what happened that day...or calling to say goodnight. The lines of communication between each parent and their children should always be open.

Telephone

We have agreed that either of us can call Grace at each other's home at any point. We have decided not to put any structure around the timeframe, or the amount of time relating to a specific call. We just try to respect the fact that the calls should be during a reasonable hour and for a reasonable amount of time. We also do not "monitor" these calls in any way.

We have also always told Grace that she can call either of us at any time.

In addition, we have encouraged family members to call Grace at either home as desired...as it is hard for extended family to keep up with where Grace is on a given day.

If your children are of the age when they can have a cell phone (and this age differs by family), needless to say, the ability to communicate with your children changes dramatically. Thanks to FaceTime and Skype there is also the ability to talk face-to-face with your children.

Messages between Parents

We agreed that we would not communicate messages to each other via Grace. If we have something we need to discuss, we call, e-mail or text each other.

We have found that depending on what we are trying to communicate...putting the message in a text or an e-mail is best, in order to have a written record of what has been discussed and/or agreed to...just in case there is a temporary memory lapse...on either side.

It can be helpful to figure out with your ex-husband how you want to handle going through the laundry list of points that you may need to discuss regarding your children. This could be a weekly or monthly call (or e-mail). Either way could work... the focus should be on ensuring you are communicating (and discussing as needed) in a productive manner all topics related to your children.

If it gets to a state where you cannot communicate directly with your ex-husband, then find a third party (e.g., your nanny) to communicate details to each other. It is important that your children are not involved in relaying messages between the two of you.

Sharing & Managing Key Situations

Throughout your children's lives, there are going to be situations that occur...whether it is at school, when they are spending time with friends, during extracurricular activities, or while hanging out at home.

One parent may be more in the know about a situation if they happened to have been there when it occurred or the children decided to confide in them about what has taken place.

Regardless, you should have an agreement with your ex-husband that you will let each other know (as quickly as possible) about what has taken place and how the situation is being addressed, so both of you can help your children deal with the situation.

Messaging with Your Child

There are a number of other points that are important to keep in mind when thinking about how you manage discussions with your children relating to the divorce.

It is important for you to determine how much you discuss the divorce proceedings with your children (it is recommended by experts that you do not discuss any details with your children). It is also recommended not to complain about, criticize or blame the other parent (or family members) in front of the children.

Inevitably, you will be asked by your children..."Why did you get a divorce?" So, you need to be prepared to discuss this question with them. Not surprisingly, your children may ask you for years the same questions about why you got divorced. It is essential to stay consistent in your answer...and, if possible, align your messaging with your ex-husband to ensure your children are not receiving different messages.

It goes without saying that going through this process is a very emotional experience that can bring out a wide range of emotions when engaging with the individual you are divorcing. However, if you can take the high road and follow these principles...it is in the best interest of your children.

Access to Records / Key Documents

There are a wide range of details you and your ex-husband will want (and need) access to throughout the time you are co-parenting your children.

This includes vaccination records, healthcare insurance claims, to school report cards, passports...and any other important documents that may be provided throughout the course of your children's lives.

It is helpful to agree who will be keeping these records, whether in paper or electronic files, so they are readily accessible as needed.

School

From a school standpoint, there are a number of things you want to ensure that you each receive.

Ensure the school lists each of you as a parent of your children.

Ensure the school is clear that both of you should receive all information and copies of any school communications relating to your children (e.g., report cards, school work, school activities, conduct issues, extracurricular activities). Also, if you or your ex-husband are communicating with teachers (or coaches), it is a good idea to copy each other on these communications.

Ensure you are clear in your agreement whether you want one or both parents to live in the specific school district where your children attend school.

Doctor

For managing your children's pediatrician, dentist, orthodontist and any other medical appointments and records, I would recommend using a similar approach to the one you take for school. Also, ensure each doctor's office knows there are two parents who both need to be kept in the loop on all details relating to your children.

Passport

For children under the age of 18, both parents are required to be in attendance when applying for a passport...which is only valid for five years (up to the age of 18).

One of the surprises I had post-divorce was when I went to get Grace a passport and I was told that her father was also required to attend. It was not enough for me to be there as her mother. It had never occurred to me to bring Grace's father with us for this process. We had actually discussed in advance that I was going to take Grace to get a passport.

Traveling to Other Countries with Your Children

One summer I decided to take Grace to Seattle and Vancouver for a summer vacation. We first flew to Seattle, then took a flight to Vancouver.

As we were going through Customs in Vancouver, the Customs Agent asked me where my daughter's father was...and I told her that we were divorced. She then turned to Grace and asked her if her father knew where she was... and Grace said, "Yes." The Customs Agent then asked for the letter from her father stating that I could take her out of the country. I told her that I did not know that was a requirement. She said it was...especially for Canada, where they have many parents from the U.S. who try to take their children from the other parent by crossing the border. I told her that was not the case in this instance...and she said that she would let us through, but that in the future I needed to have a letter from her father confirming that he was aware and supportive of the fact that she was traveling abroad with her mother.

Lesson learned...and definitely not something anyone had ever mentioned to me...so, just an important point to file away for future reference. There are examples of this type of letter and required details online for your reference.

Financial

Throughout the entire process, there are a wide range of financial details that you need to address. However, at this point, there are specific financial considerations that need to be thought through from a Parenting Plan standpoint. This ranges from child support...tax deduction considerations... healthcare... education...extracurricular activities...clothing... cell phone...computer...car...travel... allowance...and savings.

Child Support

Each U.S. state (and countries around the world) regulate the payment of child support, but different formulas are used for calculating child support.

These are details you should discuss with your attorney, who will provide you with the appropriate guidance. Based upon where you live, they may be able to inform you about potential for deviations from the standard formula.

In addition, one important point to inquire about is tax considerations for the person who is paying and receiving the child support payment.

Tax Deduction

Prior to filing taxes the first year after your divorce, you should get advice from your tax accountant regarding the best changes to make for your post-divorce tax filing process. It is important to decide which parent will claim "household" and which parent will claim "single." If you claim "household", then it should entitle you to more exemptions.

Healthcare

The cost of healthcare (physical and mental) is very important to think through in terms of how it will be covered for your children. This includes insurance, co-payments, deductibles, uninsured procedures, glasses, dental, orthodontics, counseling and other potential health-related expenses.

It is essential to confirm who will maintain the healthcare coverage and pay premiums for comprehensive healthcare for your children (through age 26, or as long as they can be covered as a dependent). Also, within your agreement, you need to clarify who will cover any uninsured medical expenses.

If both parents are working, then you can determine which company offers the better healthcare package. Based on this decision, if there is a need to change insurance companies, then ensure your doctors are covered by your new insurance... prior to making the switch.

Also, you can determine whether you will split healthcare costs for your children 50/50 (or another split) or if one of the parents will pay in full.

Generally, the ex-husband will provide healthcare coverage for the children if the mom works part-time or stays at home.

Additionally, within your agreement, it is feasible to negotiate healthcare coverage for yourself...for a reasonable period of time post-divorce. One of my girlfriends negotiated coverage for three years.

If you are able to negotiate coverage for yourself for a few years post-divorce, then it will give you time to adjust and, if needed, to find a career that offers health benefits.

Also, ensure the agreement takes into account the potential for increases in your children's healthcare costs over the years you or your ex-husband will be covering them.

Each parent should receive a copy of the healthcare card issued by the insurance company each year. It is also important to keep all records and receipts related to medical expenses, in case you need to reconcile any costs at the end of the year.

Education

There are a number of things to think through when it comes to education...costs for school tuition (if required), tutoring, college prep, music, religious, and any other educational opportunities. In addition, the decision needs to be made in terms of how to handle these higher education costs (tuition, room and board) at either a public or private university.

These decisions are obviously specific to the children, and the education options you are considering for your children...for grade school, middle school, high school and college.

It is helpful to think about and discuss these points with your soon-to-be ex-husband. If you can agree at this stage...it is preferable to discuss now versus potentially debating these points down the road. Whichever approach you take, the individual who is noted as "primary decision maker" has the final say regarding these decisions.

Private School Expenses

If you are in the situation where your children attend private schools, there are some additional expense considerations to think through.

The agreement should clearly outline who will cover private school expenses, which should be defined as (but not limited to)...private school tuition, any required fees, lunches, transportation costs, books, uniforms, field trips, summer study abroad programs, etc.

There should be a clause in the agreement that addresses what will happen if your children are unable to attend the private school that they have been attending (e.g., due to relocation)...and outline clearly defined expectations of an "equivalent" school.

College 529 Accounts

When it comes to college expenses, start by defining who will be responsible for funding (and has ownership) of 529 accounts. Ensure you have account names, account numbers and all related details are clearly outlined.

College Expenses

There are a number of things to think through relating to college expenses…tuition, room and board, books, fees, spending money, study abroad, Greek life, car at school, travel, etc.

It is important to build into your agreement an understanding of the range of college options you want to have for your children…such as a full four-year accredited private or public college, graduate school, medical or law school, etc. It is also helpful to outline how the decision of which college to attend will be made by the children and their parents.

Depending on the state (or country) you live in, the law may vary regarding what can be included within the divorce agreement relating to a parent's obligation to cover college expenses. In many states, child support is only legally required through high school and college expenses are treated as incremental (and not legally bound by child support). This is a point you will want to ask your attorney about in order to understand what is feasible to include within your divorce agreement as well as define who will cover which expenses.

Alternatives to College

If you have a child with a separate interest or talent (e.g., music, theater, sports), you could note this in your agreement...and agree on how you want to handle funding their life after high school, but before they are able to support themselves. For example, you could pay your child's expenses for four years after high school similarly to what you would pay for expenses during college.

One of my girlfriends has a daughter who has a desire to explore a career in music...which may not take her down the path of a typical four-year college experience. She has written specific language into her parental agreement to address this scenario.

Extracurricular Activities

The decision needs to be made in terms of how to handle the cost of extracurricular activities that you and your ex-husband agree your children will engage in throughout the year (including summer camps). These costs could include team fees, equipment, uniforms and travel costs.

We decided to split these costs. However, if one of us has a specific activity that we want to do with Grace, then we pay for it ourselves. For example, I take Grace with me to my Pilates 1-on-1 session and pay for her to join me...and my ex-husband decided to take ballroom dancing lessons with Grace and paid for this himself.

Clothing

As you are thinking through the approach you will take to buying clothing for your children, there is the choice of clothes they will wear...and who will pay for the clothes.

We made the decision to jointly fund Grace's clothes. We actually set-up a separate credit card for Grace's clothing purchases, so we can jointly view and manage the account together and pay the account balance as needed.

If you will be receiving child support, this may be handled differently...as you will likely be expected to allocate funds from the child support to buy clothes for your children.

Cell Phones & Computers

When your children are allowed to have their own cell phones and computers, there will be additional costs such the monthly phone bill or the replacement costs when a phone or computer is lost or broken.

Agree up front with your ex-husband how you want to handle covering these costs...as they can add up quickly depending on how responsible your children are in terms of taking care of their cell phones and computers.

Car

Before your children receive their driver's license, you and your ex-husband should discuss whether you will support your children having their own car. Once this decision is made, then the plan of how to split the related costs (e.g. cost of purchasing the car, insurance, gas, maintenance and AAA) needs to be thought through (including potentially having your child cover some or all of these costs). These costs could be defined to start at sixteen, and continue through four years after high school.

This can be a tough topic to work out in advance, but if you can align on the key decisions as part of your Parenting Plan... it will help to minimize the discussion or debate at the time your child is getting their driver's license...which is already a stressful time for parents.

Travel

Travel costs are a key point to align on with your ex-husband to ensure you are clear on how these costs will be covered for the trips your children will take throughout the year.

We agreed to cover travel for Grace from our own accounts (not Grace's joint account) for any travel we are doing with her. The only travel that is jointly covered from Grace's account is related to trips that do not involve either of us traveling with her (e.g., summer camp or school trip).

Allowance

If your children will be paid an allowance, it should be decided whether both parents will be paying an allowance...or whether one parent will take on this responsibility. The amount of the allowance should be mutually agreed to by both parents, so it is equitable if both parents are paying the children. It should also be determined how often the allowance will be paid.

One fun parenting idea...we have been paying an allowance to Grace since she was three years old. At the time, we set-up three piggy banks...one for "saving"...one for "spending"...and one for "giving." Whenever she gets her allowance, she needs to split it across the three piggy banks. We hope to teach her that she needs to think of these three areas of financial consideration as she grows older.

Savings

It is important to think through the savings you need to have for your children...whether for private school, for college (in a 529 account) or in general. Either way, the amount you want to save for your children needs to be agreed upon between you and your ex-husband.

Ideally, the agreed to amount will be paid to your children's savings account on a monthly basis via a direct deposit. This can also be handled separately by each parent. The important point is that you are setting aside savings for the major costs in your children's lives.

Miscellaneous Expenses

There are always additional expenses that come up during the time your children are spending with you or your ex-husband, so you need to define within the agreement who will cover these expenses.

For example, when your children are invited to birthday parties...who funds the gifts? If your children are at the toy store with you and want a new toy...who will fund this purchase? If your children want to take friends to a movie...who will fund this excursion? These types of scenarios come up all of the time, so it is helpful to lay out the ground rules for how these miscellaneous expenses will be funded.

Entering Each Other's Homes

It is helpful to define how you want to handle entering each other's homes...such as when your children need something from the home. If your children are young, then you may need to help them in collecting items...if the other parent is not home. Obviously, older children can go in and get what they need from the house.

It helps to define how you want to communicate with your ex-husband if/when you need to enter his home, or vice versa. We agreed that we would text each other and ensure there is a reply of approval in advance of ever entering the other person's home.

There are instances when this dynamic may not be feasible. If this is the case in your situation, then try to protect your space without causing undue stress for your children when they need something from one of your homes.

Leaving Children by Themselves

It is important to discuss and align on the specific age at which you are comfortable leaving your children alone at home, and under what circumstances (during the day, at night, overnight).

Depending on the ages of your children, this may or may not be a consideration for you as you are thinking about how you will be parenting at both households. However, it is an important point to think through, so you are being consistent at both households.

Leaving Children with Other Adults

It is important to outline expectations regarding with whom your children can be left during custodial visits.

For example, during time meant to be spent with their father, will it be acceptable for your children to stay with their paternal grandparents, paternal aunts and uncles, friends or your ex-husband's significant other?

Just remember that the guidelines you put in place are reciprocal, so you will need to adhere to the same guidelines you put in place for your ex-husband.

Work-Related Travel

If one or both of you travel for work, you may want to think through the impact your work travel will have on your family...and adjust as necessary to ensure the time you are each spending with your children is aligned to what has been agreed to in your Parenting Plan.

It is possible to add a "first right of refusal" into your agreement, so that if one of you is traveling, the other one has the opportunity to have the kids...before having a nanny, family member or friends watch the kids while you are out of town.

Family Pets

If there are pets in your household, you will to need to think through how you want to handle the pets post-divorce. One parent may end up having the pet live with them. There is also the scenario where the pet transitions with the children to each household.

Overnight Dates

It is important to define how you want to handle whether you or your ex-husband will have a boyfriend, girlfriend or any other guest (who is unrelated by blood or marriage) spend the night when the children are at your home.

Generally, this may be referred to in the legal agreement as a "morality clause," which clearly outlines these expectations in this scenario.

Moving

If you potentially intend to move away from the place where you are currently living...especially if you are considering moving across state lines (or out of the country), then it is recommended that you clearly define what this means in terms of the custody agreement with your ex-husband. Depending on the state (or country) you are living in, there are specific considerations that you may need to think through regarding moving your children away from their father.

If this is a consideration for you, research the state (or country) guidelines and requirements for where you are living in order to be well informed on your options relating to this point.

Co-Parenting

For reference, the term "co-parenting" basically means that each of you are contributing to being a parent to your children...and trying to work together as parents to ensure the best decisions are made on behalf of your children.

In general, we have agreed to a co-parenting approach that is based on the spirit of reasonable flexibility.

Each point outlined in the Parenting Plan is very specific to a given family, so you just need to make the best decisions you can at the time of your divorce...and accept the fact that if certain aspects of your life or your ex-husband's life change, you may need to revisit points. However, in general, you now have a roadmap for how the two of you will co-parent your children moving forward.

The goal as you are going through your divorce is to try to continue a co-parenting relationship with your ex-husband that focuses on your children...as you will be co-parenting with him for years to come.

One important point in terms of co-parenting is to always try to back each other up...when it comes to decisions you have jointly made about raising your children. This is an important principle to align on...because even when parents are together, children can try to play one off of the other. In a divorce scenario, there is even more potential for this to happen, so agreeing that you will always try to back each other up is a great starting point for the approach you will take to co-parenting.

One of my girlfriend's shared, "At the end of the day, hopefully we both can keep in mind the dreams we had for our children, the values we want to instill in them, and the expectations we had for them when we were married...and stay true to them even though we are now divorced."

Creating Two Homes

As you are going through the shift to having your children live in two different places, there is a need to ensure they are equally comfortable in both homes. Basically, wherever your children are staying should feel like their home.

If there is a way to ensure there are familiar family mementos (e.g., family photos, children's artwork) at both locations, it helps each house to truly feel like "home" for your children.

Create a Home Base

Even in joint custody scenarios, I would recommend making one of the houses "home base." What this actually means is that you define which home your children will go to every day after school and where they will spend the majority of their days during the summer. The reason we have found this helpful is that it does provide consistency for Grace on a daily basis...as well as for her friends...to know where she will be each day.

This does not mean that the other home is not a "home" for the children. It is important for the children to feel at home whether they are staying with their mother or their father... and if managed well, this is feasible.

One of my girlfriends (who has two children) shared that her children have reacted very differently to their new living arrangements. One child is fine with going back and forth between homes as needed due to the custody agreement and one child prefers having a "home base" at her house. If you have children with different personalities, then you will need to determine whether establishing a home base makes sense (or not).

There are also situations where children are in daycare or attend after-school activities and will be picked up by the parent who has custody that day. This means there may not be an opportunity to establish a consistent "home base" depending on how the children's days are structured.

Create the Space You Want to Live In

Whether you decide to stay in the house you have been living in prior to divorce or you are moving into a new place... take the time and create the space you want to live in after your divorce.

In the past, you may have been making joint house-related decisions with your husband. These decisions are now for you to make...with your children's input, as appropriate. This is an opportunity to think about the environment you want to create...the style and colors you like...creating a space that truly reflects you and the environment you want to create for your family.

There is also the consideration of whether to keep or remove mementos from your marriage, such as wedding photos, or gifts from your ex-husband. This is a personal decision you will need to think through in terms of whether these items still can bring a smile to your face when you see them in your home.

Speaking from experience, I decided to redecorate my house as I was going through the divorce, so that once the process was finished...it would feel like my place.

One of the things I did was transform our living room (which used to be very dark and more masculine in look and feel) into a relaxing space that my girlfriends affectionately refer to as the "Spa Room." It is a place where I now relax with friends and talk about a wide range of topics. The irony is that this is a room that we rarely used when I was married...and it is now my favorite room in the house.

I also redecorated my bedroom with all new bedding which helped to transition the bedroom from a room I had shared with my ex-husband into my room.

It is also important to ensure your children's rooms are places that they are excited about spending time in...as there can be the potential for "competition of the rooms" at each house. When my ex-husband bought his house, he allowed Grace to paint her room any color she wanted, so she painted it purple...this became a joke between us because she knows I hate the color purple. I told her that it was great that she could have a purple room at her dad's house.

I have to admit that it was fascinating for me to see the change...both in my house, and in the reaction others have when they come over post-divorce. It is now a very calm and relaxing place. After the divorce, I actually felt a weight had been lifted off of me and the house...which is reflected from both a decorating standpoint and the feeling you have when you walk in the front door. Even though I remained in the house that we had lived in together, it feels completely different and it now reflects how I am feeling...at peace with my new life.

If you end up moving to a new place, think about the essentials that you want and need to have in order to make a place feel like a home for you and your children.

Minimize the Gaps

When you are going through a divorce, there is the inevitable need to divide up belongings between yourself and your spouse. One of the efforts I made during our divorce was to make sure that for any piece of furniture or painting going with my ex-husband...I had a replacement item ready to put in its place when that item was removed.

The reason this was so important to me was because I was going to be staying in the house with Grace...so I did not want her to see her environment being pulled apart...leaving gaps in the house that had not been there before the divorce.

This may sound challenging, considering everything else you are juggling during a divorce...but I found it to be a very important and helpful step to maintain a sense of visual order in Grace's life...and not have it appear that everything was being torn apart.

An example is that we had a wall of black-and-white family photographs that ran the length of our downstairs hallway. It was a combination of old photos from my family and my ex-husband's family. As we were going through the divorce, I made the effort to frame other black-and-white photos of Grace, myself, and my family that I would put on the wall to replace my ex-husband's family photos (as he would be taking these with him). I decided to replace the framed photos on the wall on a day when Grace was across the street at a friend's house. When Grace arrived home, within minutes of being back in the house, she said, "Mom, the hallway wall has changed..." and I asked what had been changed and she said,

"There are more photos of me up there now...it looks great." She had not noticed that all of her father's family photos had been removed. This was in part due to her age...and in part due to the fact that she was right...there were a lot more photos of her on the wall. Regardless, it was amazing to me that she had noticed this change in her environment so quickly.

This is why we cannot underestimate the impact the environment we create for our children has on them, and why we should try to minimize the appearance that it is being pulled apart due to the divorce.

Prepare the Professional Traveler

When you are thinking through the decision of how to structure your children's lives, there are so many considerations... many of which depend on whether you are going to have sole custody or joint custody.

Either way (sole custody or joint custody)...the hardest thing I was told when I was going through my divorce came from our child specialist, whom we met with in advance of having Grace see him.

He asked me if I traveled, and I said, "Yes, I travel internationally for my job." He asked my ex-husband, and he said, "Yes, I travel domestically for my job." Then, the child specialist said, "Well, Grace has just become a professional traveler...she is going to travel back and forth between your two homes for the next eleven years." At that point, I burst into tears because the reality was setting in that regardless of the reasons why we were getting a divorce...Grace was going to be the one most impacted by our decision.

So, at that point we made a couple of decisions...and I appreciate that what I am going to share with you is dependent on the fact that we could afford to take this approach. However, I can share with you five years after the fact...I fundamentally believe that some of the decisions we have made regarding Grace's day-to-day schedule and routine have made a big difference in terms of her ability to adjust to the significant change we put her through due to the divorce.

Set a Goal to Never Pack a Bag

Even though Grace was about to become a professional traveler for the next eleven years...another principle that we have tried to live by is that Grace never has to pack a bag when going between our homes. The only things that travel back and forth with her are her backpack for school, and her golf bag (on the days she has golf lessons).

Logistically, what this means is that we buy two of everything for Grace, so that she has clothes at both homes. I completely appreciate that this is not always feasible from a financial standpoint. However, if you are able to set-up your children's lives at both homes...so they do not need to pack a bag...then you are minimizing the "professional traveler" dynamic that will be a reality for your children.

A by-product of this approach is that one house can end up with more jeans, t-shirts and socks than the other house. When this happens, it is up to my ex-husband and me to even out the clothes and figure out if some of the clothes need to be taken to the other house. We have never asked Grace to manage this process, because we believe it is not her responsibility to ensure she has clothes at both homes...it is ours.

Always be mindful of which items are special and/or important to your children...and ensure those items are with them wherever they are staying. It is not your children's fault that they do not have that one special item at both houses, so I would recommend figuring out how to transition these items without involving your children.

If you have a nanny who is involved in both homes, you could have your nanny help with any items that need to be transitioned between homes. Ideally, the nanny would handle the packing and unpacking of overnight bags (if required) while the children are not home, so they do not have to see their things being transitioned.

It is already stressful enough for our children to keep up with all of the details of their day-to-day lives...in terms of homework, books, laptop and phone...the additional requirement of keeping up with the basics to live their lives (clothes, toiletries, etc.) should not be something they have to be concerned with on a day-to-day basis.

As your children become teens, they will start to take things to or from each home and will not want their parents involved in helping them. However, even as Grace has gotten older, we still try to even out the "clothes balance" when we see that more of a certain item of clothing is at one of our houses.

The goal of "never packing a bag" could be setting the bar too high...a more realistic goal may be to "minimize packing." Regardless, be conscious of the impact that packing a bag each week can have on your children, and work to find ways to minimize this dynamic.

Transition of Special Items & Miscellaneous Stuff

Whether or not you achieve the goal of "never packing a bag"...there are still special items and miscellaneous stuff that need to go back and forth with your children between homes each week, whether it is a special blanket, stuffed animal or sports equipment. It is important to determine how these items will be transitioned between homes...and whether or not your children are required to be accountable for helping to transition these items...or whether you will handle the transition for them.

Early on post-divorce, I decided to set aside a shelf in our hallway cupboard for the smaller "special" items as well as the other miscellaneous items that may have needed to go to my ex-husband's house. This ensures there is one spot my ex-husband can go to in order to check to see if there is anything that needs to go to his house. It also is used for anything he needs to drop off at my house. This has actually been helpful for both of us to stay organized with the things we have needed to transition between our homes.

Create a Family Calendar

When trying to manage your children's lives across two house-holds...it is helpful to keep one calendar that both parents (and nanny...if one is involved in your children's lives) can view and manage as needed. This way each parent can work off the same understanding of where the children are each day...as well as keeping everything straight in terms of school and extracurricular activities.

A Google calendar has worked well for us. We all have access to it (including our nanny), but there are many calendar options these days that can help a family manage these details.

We generally end up having a call about once a month to run through calendar-related items. This ensures we are aligned on any changes or shifts that are taking place in the calendar. We have also found it helpful to outline any specific requests for key calendar shifts via e-mail, so we can keep track of what we have collectively agreed to when dates change.

Some families have a major need for this type of calendar to manage all of the details...especially when multiple children are involved, with a wide range of activities taking place on a day-to-day basis. While this may not be needed for certain families, if you are co-parenting and/or there is a nanny involved in helping to manage your children's schedules, this approach to managing the calendar works very well to ensure everyone is clear on what is happening in your children's lives...and when.

Ensure Childcare & Household Support is in Place

One of the essential considerations when becoming a single mom is to have the right childcare support in place after the divorce. Whether you are a stay-at-home mom or a working mom...do not underestimate your need for support.

The first thing to determine is what level of childcare support you need, which may be different due to the divorce.

From our standpoint, we have always had a nanny (since Grace was twelve weeks old). However, because of the divorce we now needed a nanny with some additional considerations. She needed to understand we were co-parenting in a divorced situation, so she needed to be able to watch Grace at my house and at my ex-husband's house as needed.

There also may be daycare, after-school programs, relatives, friends or nanny-share scenarios...there are many options for support. Just recognize that you will need help, so you will just need to figure out the best scenario that works for you.

In addition, there is also a need for additional "support" with the house...so if you are hiring a nanny...consider hiring a nanny who is also capable of being a "house manager." They should be able to handle errands, dry cleaners, managing home repair appointments, etc...whatever it is you need to make your life work on a daily basis. This is essential when you are trying to juggle raising your children, running a household on your own and potentially a career as well.

Hiring & Managing a Nanny

We had also made the decision that we would share a nanny versus hiring a different one at each household. We have found this to be very helpful, as it has ensured consistency in Grace's life on a day-to-day basis...and provided continuity across both of our households.

In terms of actually interviewing and making a final decision on the nanny, we have always interviewed for a new nanny together. This was the case before the divorce, and we have continued this approach post-divorce. This ensures we are both comfortable with the individual who will be spending time with Grace...and that they can work for each of us.

We have also always included Grace in the nanny interviewing process...as we think it is most important that she has a say in who she will be spending time with each day.

It is important to agree on who will manage your nanny in terms of confirming hours, paying each week and communicating children's activity schedules.

Also, try not to put your nanny in the middle of discussions between you and your ex-husband. The nanny's focus should be on helping with your children.

Organize Details to Keep Your Life Running

There is a wide range of details that you need to ensure are in order relating to keeping your life running on a day-to-day basis. Some relate to the divorce...and some are just those things necessary for managing our households and our lives.

As you organize these details, ensure you keep all of the key documents in a central place that you can access easily, as you will end up needing to refer to them a lot during the first few post-divorce years.

Determine Alimony

Depending on your financial situation, it will need to be determined whether alimony is part of your settlement agreement. The rules relating to how much alimony...and the time period for receiving it...will be defined based on the state (or country) you live in at the time of your divorce. The attorney you hire will be able to provide you with the required guidance on this topic. However, there are some key points for you to keep in mind...

It is important to ask about tax considerations relating to alimony. In certain states, alimony (unlike childcare) is taxable to the individual receiving the alimony, so you should take this into consideration when defining the alimony amount.

Also, one of my girlfriends negotiated a sliding scale for her alimony amount that was due to the possible change in her ex-husband's earning potential.

Alimony should take into account if your ex-husband has an equity interest in a business or startup, law firm, medical practice, etc.

If there is a bonus your ex-husband will have earned during your marriage, but the payout of this bonus will take place once divorce proceedings have begun...you should ask for your fair share of the earned bonus.

It is important to ensure your agreement states that dollars invested in life insurance payments are not to be considered part of alimony.

A final point to remember is that alimony generally stops if you get remarried.

Divide Up Assets

Depending on your situation, you will need to determine how you want to divide up your assets...which could include finances (such as stocks or bonds), properties, cars, club memberships, furniture, etc.

As you are thinking through these details, outline the time-frame for when you want the division of assets completed.

It is actually important to inventory everything in your house, so that when it comes time to divide up household belongings with your spouse...you have a clear understanding of the items...and the value of each item. This sounds like a tedious task (which it definitely is)...but it is a necessary and important task to ensure you are clear on the value of the items you will be dividing up with your spouse, or keeping for yourself.

If there are items that you owned prior to your marriage, or inherited during your marriage that have special meaning to you, ensure you have thought through how you want to handle these items as you are dividing up your assets.

Retirement Savings

Ensure you have a list of all retirement savings accounts, and have divided them up appropriately.

One of my girlfriends made this suggestion based on the guidance she received during her divorce, "If the retirement settlement amount is a set amount, open up a rollover IRA and quickly move the retirement amount into this account. If you do not use this approach, the interest will be going to your ex-husband's account."

There is also the need to be clear on who is the beneficiary of each retirement account (yours and your ex-husband's). One of my girlfriends negotiated that if her ex-husband passed away after the divorce, she would receive funds from the specific retirement account...in order to ensure her children would receive these funds.

Debt

If you and your ex-husband are entering into the process with any debt, you need to confirm who will pay off any outstanding debt (e.g., credit cards, home equity loans, school loans) that has been incurred during your marriage.

Tax Return Refund

If there is a tax return refund that will be coming back during the process, you need to define how you will handle dividing up the refund.

Air Miles

If one or both of you travel extensively for business, the air miles that you are able to use for personal travel could be significant. Depending on your situation, it may make sense to address how you want to handle your air miles (with all airline carriers where accounts exist).

My friend's husband had accumulated a large number of air miles due to their travel that she negotiated to be divided up as part of her divorce agreement.

To Change Your Name (or Not)

The decision of whether to change your name back to your maiden name (if you changed your name when you got married) is a very personal decision.

Some of my girlfriends have gone back to their maiden name, and some friends have stayed with their married names. I actually decided to stay with my married name, as I was too established in my career to change my name post-divorce.

Changing your name can be done at any time. However, if you think you are going to change your name, it may make sense to do so before going through all of the required administrative changes in your life (e.g., changing names on bills, insurance coverage, wills).

Divorce Agreement & Divorce Decree

There are generally two separate documents which are required to finalize your divorce from a legal standpoint...the Divorce Agreement and the Divorce Decree.

The Divorce Agreement (which may be referred to as Divorce Settlement Agreement or Marital Settlement Agreement) includes the details regarding custody, child support, alimony, and division of property/assets. This agreement should also reflect details from your Parenting Plan which have been agreed to between you and your ex-husband.

The Divorce Decree (which may be referred to as Final Decree, Final Divorce Decree, Final Order or Final Divorce Judgment and Order) is issued after the divorce is deemed final by the court, so it is the official confirmation that you are divorced.

If you have decided to change your name, then you should ask your attorney if this change can be incorporated into the Divorce Decree.

After your divorce is final, there will be instances when you may be asked to provide a certified copy of your Divorce Decree to confirm that you are officially divorced (e.g., when changing names on bills). Ensure you have all legal documents related to your divorce in electronic versions as well as certified copies, so you can share as needed post-divorce.

Open Checking & Savings Accounts

It will be important to ensure you have the right bank accounts set-up at the stage when you are ready to separate your finances (if they have not been separate during your marriage).

The starting point is to open checking and savings accounts over which you have total control. Ideally, this is at the same bank where you are opening the joint account with your ex-husband for your children's financial support (if you decided to set one up). This will make it easier to transfer funds across accounts and have everything in one view from an online banking standpoint.

Create Joint Account for Children's Financial Support

If you are in a situation where you are jointly funding your children's lives with your ex-husband, then you may want to consider setting up a joint account. We found it to be helpful to have one account that we jointly fund (and have access to), so each month we deposit a set amount into Grace's account.

There is also the scenario where you may end up receiving child support from your ex-husband. If this is the case, then creating a jointly funded account would not be necessary. However, I would still recommend a separate account for managing your children's expenses...as it will help to clearly define that you have the appropriate funds available to support your children's lives.

If you decide to set-up a joint account, then this account also has a debit card attached to it that we have given to our nanny for any expenses that come up during a given week.

In addition, we have a separate credit card that we use for Grace's major expenses (clothes, golf lessons or other big purchases). We then jointly pay off this credit card, as needed.

There may be the need to agree on how much you will be "jointly" spending in certain areas...for example, children's clothes...as this can become a point of contention if not discussed and agreed upon in advance.

This approach has enabled us to have a very clear view of the expenses related to Grace's life and to manage these details with full transparency throughout the year. Due to this approach, there has never been a debate on how we are spending the money that is in Grace's account.

Apply for Your Own Credit Cards

If you already have credit cards that are not linked to your ex-husband, then this will not be necessary. However, if all of your credit cards are joint, then you need to apply for credit cards that are only in your name.

I have actually found it helpful to have two separate credit cards...

I have one credit card for day-to-day expenses. I also give my nanny this same card for any errands she runs on my behalf.

In addition, I have a credit card for my major expenses, such as furniture, travel and clothes. This helps me to keep a clear view of how I am spending money that could be seen as "discretionary", so I can manage these expenses separately from my day-to-day expenses.

Develop Your Own Credit Rating

This is an important point...especially if you are planning to apply for a mortgage or home equity line of credit.

It was not until we went through our divorce that I realized that all of our credit cards were joint. My ex-husband was the primary card holder which meant that my credit rating was not well established.

Again, this is one of those things you do not think about when you get married assuming you will be married for the long term, but it is essential to have your own credit rating established.

Change Name on Bills

When it comes time to change the bills into your name, set aside the required time to handle these details. This can be more time consuming than you think...and in many instances, the company (whether it is phone, cable, electric, gas, etc.) will request proof of the change of ownership of the home. For example, they may request a copy of your divorce decree in order to change bills into your name.

Understand Mortgage Details

If you are staying in the home that you have been living in, ensure you are clear on where things stand with the current mortgage on your house.

To start, get clear on who has the right, title and interest related to your home.

Also, check with your mortgage broker to understand what is required to obtain a "quitclaim deed" in order to take over the mortgage (if this is what will be taking place relating to your mortgage).

If you are not working (or even if you are) and you need to refinance, then you need to agree upon a reasonable amount of time to refinance...ideally, within 24 months of your divorce being final.

It is also important to establish a relationship with a trusted mortgage broker who can keep you connected to what is happening in the market, including interest rates. There may be opportunities over the course of time for you to refinance your mortgage, so having a good mortgage broker who can highlight these windows of opportunity for you can be helpful.

As with other financial matters during our marriage, I had always left managing the mortgage details to my ex-husband. So, during the process, I was also getting a crash course on mortgages from my mortgage broker who was very patient with me as I asked him a wide range of questions.

Understand Insurance Coverage

Whether or not you were handling these details during your marriage will determine whether you need to educate yourself on the type of insurance coverage you have in place...from homeowners, to auto, personal liability umbrella, jewelry... and the list can go on...

This is a topic that requires you to find time to call your insurance agent and walk through the details of your coverage to ensure it accurately reflects your needs for the future.

Change Health Insurance

If your health insurance is tied to your employer, then you will need to update your health insurance coverage to ensure it just covers you and your children.

However, if you are currently a stay-at-home mom, you need to determine how you will handle health insurance coverage once the divorce is final.

Change Will & Living Will

If you have a joint will with your ex-husband, you will need to ensure that you create a separate will that clearly states your intentions and confirms beneficiaries.

In addition, if you have a living will, you need to ensure the appropriate individual is noted to make any decisions on your behalf, if the situation arises.

If you do not have a will (and living will), then ask friends for a referral and get started on putting a will (and living will) in place during or soon after the divorce is final.

Confirm Life Insurance Beneficiary

If you have life insurance, you will need to ensure the beneficiary noted in your life insurance is changed...if your ex-husband has been your beneficiary.

One of my girlfriends negotiated into her agreement that if her ex-husband were to pass away, she would be the beneficiary of her ex-husband's life insurance...to enable her to care for their children, as outlined in their agreement.

Hire an Accountant

There will be a point where you will need to decide if you need an accountant to help you file your taxes, and provide advice regarding filing separately...unless you are already handling filing your taxes yourself, and are clear on the tax guidance relating to filing.

If you need to find an accountant, ask your friends for recommendations.

Engage a Financial Planner

From a financial planning standpoint, confirm who you want to use for a financial planner. If you and your husband have already been working with a financial planner, determine if you want to continue working with this individual or find a separate financial planner for your discussions.

In some instances, it could be helpful to remain with the same financial planner. In other instances, it may be best to have separate advice on the topic. This is a decision you will have to make based on your circumstances.

Again, if you need to find a financial planner, ask your friends for recommendations. Once you have a list of recommendations, set up brief phone interviews to see if they are the right fit for your financial planning needs.

POST the CHANGE

Prepare for a Year of Firsts

The first year after your divorce is final can be a hard year. It will also be a year of firsts...and with every first...whether it is first holiday, birthday, parent-teacher conference, school play, sporting event, family vacation...whatever it is...reflect on that first and decide whether you want to repeat the way you approached it...and decide if there is anything you will never repeat again.

The good news is that the "Year of Firsts" is only one year, but it is a year you should learn from...as it will help you define how you want to live your life in this next phase you are entering post-divorce.

Recover from Divorce Hangover

I was talking to one of my girlfriends, who had also recently gone through a divorce. She said that she was still working through things, and I said, "Everyone's divorce hangover is different...some take longer than others to recover...and there is an emotional headache that you need to recover from...but you eventually will...and will move on with your life."

Another girlfriend shared that she thought to herself, "I could be one of those women who spends one to two years getting over the trauma of a divorce, or I can make the conscious decision to walk through this process as healthy and strong as possible...so at the end, I am standing with my two feet on the ground...even if my knees are a bit wobbly from the journey."

Understand that Everyone Takes a Side (Even If You Don't Ask Them To)

We actually had an amicable divorce...but, even in this instance, our friends ended up taking sides...not because either of us asked them to take sides...but because this naturally occurs during a divorce.

This came as a surprise to me...as I had not wanted this to be the case...but what I realized from this situation is that even if you have an amicable divorce...you cannot control how other people will react in these situations. It is important to respect the fact that everyone (family and friends) handles divorce in their own way. The only thing you can control is how you approach it for yourself and your children.

There are a couple of places where this change in your life will start to become clear. One is invitations for friends' dinner parties and events that you receive (or do not receive)... and the other is whether you are kept on the holiday card list of your ex-husband's friends. Again...not a big deal...but there are those individuals who feel the need to take sides, even when you have not asked them to take a side. In these instances, decide who is genuinely important for you to stay in contact with...and then make the effort to stay in contact with them...whether by sending them a holiday card or inviting them over for dinner.

Ironically, in this very personal situation you are going through, when these things occur, you should try not to take them personally. It is actually not personal...it is a social dynamic that no one truly knows how to handle, and they do the best they can...without knowing whether they are handling it appropriately or not.

Spending Quality Time with Your Children

As you enter into your post-divorce phase, ensure you are spending quality time with your children. How you define "quality time" will depend on the age of your children. This is a time when your children will be assessing this new phase of life...and you want them to know that the time you are spending with them is a priority.

This can be a challenge, given the long list of things you are most likely juggling at this stage, but it is important to put away your laptop, cell phone or "to do" list...whatever is distracting you...and focus on spending quality time with your children.

Helping with Homework

It is helpful to define the approach you want to take in terms of how your children will handle finishing their homework each day. This means thinking through where and when they will complete their homework, and who will help them. This sounds straightforward, but when children are transitioning between homes, it is important to be clear on which parent is accountable for ensuring the homework is completed on any given day.

Attending Parent-Teacher Conferences

If possible, it is helpful for the two of you to attend parent-teacher conferences together, as this enables you to show to the teachers that both of you are involved in your children's lives...and even though you are divorced, your children are the priority.

We have always attended Grace's parent-teacher conferences together. In fact, at Grace's school, she also attends the conferences, so she has also been able to see that we are both there for her and want to engage with her teachers on how she is doing in school.

When Grace was in sixth grade we went to a parent-teacher conference together. At this point, we had been divorced for five years. At the end of the conference, the teacher asked, "Are you two divorced?" When we answered, "yes", she was shocked as she had no idea. The teacher shared that she had been in many situations where two parents could not come to the same conference to discuss their children, which she found to be a sad situation...that even when it came to discussing the one thing a divorced couple have in common... they could not spend that one hour in the room together.

Reviewing Report Cards

We sit down together with Grace when her report cards come out from school and discuss the details with her. Again, this has shown Grace that we are both there for her, especially when discussing these types of important topics.

One of my friends shared that she and her ex-husband review report cards separately with their children. However, they set aside time for a phone call to discuss 'parent to parent' any concerns, issues or themes that are being highlighted that they want to address with their children (or the children's teachers).

Keeping Up with School Details (Two Copies of Everything)

When children are in preschool and grade school there are a lot of things that are sent home in hard copy. We requested from Grace's teachers that they send home two copies of any paperwork whenever possible, so that both of us can review the details. When children are older, most of the correspondence from school is via e-mail, so this will no longer be a need.

Art projects present a unique challenge, since your child will generally only make one piece of art for a school art project.

We have tried to ensure that Grace's art pieces over the years are split up...some are at my house and some are at my ex-husband's house. In fact, many of the "gifts" Grace has given to her father over the years have been framed pieces of art she made at school.

Attending Children's Sporting Events & Activities

One of the opportunities to show support for your children is when you are attending their sporting events or activities (such as a school play or musical performance).

There is potential for a wide range of dynamics to take place at these activities, especially when you and/or your ex-husband have a significant other who is also in attendance. Hopefully, the focus at these events will be what is best for your children.

Generally, we make an effort to sit together at Grace's sporting events and school activities. We might not accomplish this at every game, but we do so when possible. Early on in our divorce, I think this confused people...but the only one we worried about confusing was Grace...and we felt she deserved to look out and see both of us sitting there together, smiling at her.

Defining Rules of Engagement for Cell Phones

There are a number of points to think through and align on when it comes to cell phones.

The first is at what age your children are allowed to get a cell phone. This is a decision both parents should make together.

Also, if there are certain rules that you want to have your children agree to in terms of cell phone usage, then you and your ex-husband should agree on these points together with your children to ensure there will be consistency in what is allowed (and not allowed) at both homes.

We actually asked Grace to write a cell phone contract which outlined the rules of engagement relating to use of her cell phone. We wanted to ensure that Grace fully understood that having a cell phone is a responsibility and a privilege... not a given.

If your child's phone is taken away as punishment, then ensure the other parent knows this is the case.

Monitoring Computer Time

The approach you and your ex-husband take to computer access for your children is also a point you should align on in order to be as consistent as possible.

For example, if at one home there is a time limit to "computer time" for your children and at the other home your children can be on the computer as long as they like...this can be both confusing and challenging for the parent that has tried to place limitations on computer usage.

As parents in this digital age, we are all trying to figure out the balance of what is acceptable and appropriate for our children in terms of how much time they spend on a computer. This is not an easy part of parenting to manage...even when a family is under one roof. When children are living in two households, it becomes even more challenging to figure out the right approach to managing this aspect of your children's lives.

Helping Your Children with Gift Giving for Your Ex-Husband

There will be several times during the year when you will need to think through how you want to handle helping your children pick out and pay for gifts for their father (for Father's Day, birthday and holiday gifts).

There are a number of ways you can handle this...

- Help your children think through gift ideas for their father and purchase and wrap them (with your children helping with the gift wrapping...regardless of age).
- Delegate to your nanny or another family member to help your children with gift ideas, purchase and wrapping of gifts.
- Leave it to your children to figure it out (depending on the age of the children, this may be an option).

Regardless of which option you choose, admittedly, this can be a challenging scenario to maneuver. The most important point is to help your children feel good about how they are recognizing their father for the special occasion...and also teaching them the valuable lesson of giving (versus receiving) gifts.

If you are in an amicable situation, then it is beneficial to align with your ex-husband on how you both want to handle gift-giving to each other from your children, so it is handled in a similar fashion in both homes. Also, this hopefully ensures that you do not go through a birthday or holiday without any special recognition from your children.

Actually, I have always told Grace that she does not need to buy me a gift, but that I would like her to be thoughtful when it comes to figuring out a gift to give me for a special occasion. For example, she has made me coupons for movie nights at the house, a coupon for "tech support" (since I can be technologically challenged at times), or a promise to go on long walks in the neighborhood together. I would much prefer to have these types of gifts from Grace than anything she could ever buy for me.

Planning & Attending Birthday Parties

The celebration of your children's birthdays is a time when, hopefully, you and your ex-husband can collectively celebrate your child's special day.

However, when it comes to a post-divorce birthday celebration for your children, there are considerations which need to be thought through...

Where will the birthday party take place? Who attends...from a parent and significant other standpoint? Who funds the party? Are gifts given from both parents or does each parent buy their own gifts? Who funds the gifts?

Some of these questions could be aligned on and included in the Parenting Plan...and others will need to be addressed at the time of the specific birthday.

Regardless of when these details are confirmed, the goal should be to create positive memories for your children relating to these special birthday celebrations.

Displaying Photos of Ex-Husband

Give this some thought, as it can definitely provide a positive signal to your children that even though you are divorced, your ex-husband is still their father. Having a picture of him in your children's rooms can show that this will always be the case.

I completely appreciate that given the dynamics of certain divorces, this may seem like a tough thing to consider, so you will have to be the judge of whether this would be seen as a positive sign by your children.

In my situation, I decided to do a wall of family photos in Grace's room that has both sides of our family represented, so Grace can look up at any point and see her family (from both sides) smiling and enjoying special memories together.

Take the High Road

There will be moments when you are frustrated by a specific dynamic with your ex-husband. This is completely normal, but as much as you can, try to take the high road. It is not always the easiest path to take...and there are times when you may question whether it is the right thing to do...but it is usually worth it in the end.

Engaging with Ex-Husband for Co-Parenting

There are many approaches couples take when engaging with each other post-divorce, so think about how you want to engage with your ex-husband from a co-parenting standpoint... and how you want to manage your children's lives with him.

I can only speak from my experience, but I have found that it works best if I only engage with my ex-husband as needed, and only in relation to the co-parenting of Grace. This is generally in the form of texts or e-mails or in conversations at one of Grace's sporting events. On a monthly basis, we may need to have a brief, half-hour phone call to discuss a list of topics relating to Grace. I actually keep a running list of topics I need to discuss with my ex-husband that are not time-sensitive, so when we do connect...we can quickly run through the points we need to discuss.

Don't Ask Questions You Don't Care About

There is also a decision you have to make in terms of how you want to interact with your ex-husband beyond co-parenting. I have certain friends who speak to their ex-husbands three times a day...and I have other friends who do not speak to them at all beyond discussions relating to co-parenting. Just think through if you want to ask any questions beyond what you need to know about your children. This is a personal choice in terms of the type of relationship you want to have or are able to have with your ex-husband.

Decide How to Engage (or Not) with Significant Others

What type of relationship you choose to have with your ex-husband's significant other is a very personal decision...and you may find you have very strong emotions when it comes to this topic...so figure out what you can handle.

My ex-husband was dating right after our divorce was final... and he very quickly had a girlfriend. My one request was that I have the opportunity to meet his girlfriend, if she was going to be spending time with Grace, so I met her for a drink. This helped me to understand the individual that would be interacting with my daughter on a regular basis.

The most important consideration is how this individual interacts with your children, and whether you are comfortable with them spending time with your children.

Children Engaging with Signficant Others

First of all, the reality is that you may not be given a choice as to when your children will start to engage with your ex-husband's significant other.

If you are able to discuss this point with your ex-husband, then the key question is...what is the appropriate timeframe to introduce your children to either your ex-husband's girl-friend or your boyfriend? Either way, these situations need to be thought through and handled carefully when children are involved.

Engaging with Your Ex-In-Laws

Depending on your situation, the relationship with your in-laws can either continue to be a positive relationship post-divorce or you may be in a situation where you will no longer engage with them once the divorce is final.

Some of my girlfriends continue to have a close relationship with their ex-in-laws. They are invited to family functions and even receive birthday gifts. In other instances, my girlfriends have not heard from their in-laws, since their divorce process started.

It is important to remember that your ex-in-laws are still your children's grandparents. If it is possible for you to maintain a relationship with them, then it only helps your children in their interactions with their grandparents over the years.

Be Mindful of Impact of Social Media

The reality of today's world is that there are a wide range of ways to share what is going on in our lives...and this is an understatement.

If you and your ex-husband can be mindful of the fact that your children and your children's friends will potentially see everything you post on social media...whether you think they will see it or not. This can help to avoid awkward and potentially hurtful situations for your children who may not have caught up to the stage of life you and your ex-husband have embarked on in your post-divorce phase.

Think About How You Want to Live Life as the New Single You

After your divorce is final, take the opportunity to reflect on how you want to live your life...as the new "single" you. This is a very personal reflection. It could be that you consider new interests or hobbies that you want to spend your time on...or a new non-profit that you want to get involved with in your community...or you want to travel more, to see friends and family. It actually can be an exciting time to think about the possibilities...and enjoy some new experiences as you start a new phase in your life.

Think About What Makes You Feel Good

There are many ways you can approach making yourself feel good in a post-divorce era.

From my standpoint, I did a couple of things...such as cleaning out the clutter, designing a special piece of jewelry, treating myself to some retail therapy and focusing on being social. Some of my friends discovered new talents...such as learning to paint...which have been fulfilling to them.

It is up to you to determine what you want to focus on to help you feel good after this significant change in your life.

Clean out the Clutter

After my divorce, I took some time over the first couple of years to clean out the clutter in our house...beyond what had been done when my ex-husband moved out.

It takes time to clean out the clutter...and it also takes the ability to let things go...

I do not recommend cleaning things out if you still are feeling emotional about the change you have gone through...as the decision of what to give away (or throw away) and what to keep is definitely impacted by your emotional state. If you think you may regret the decisions you will make in terms of what you get rid of...then I recommend waiting until you feel that you are in a good place and can objectively make decisions about how you want to handle the clutter...in your closets, drawers, basement or garage.

It may help to have a best friend or a family member join you in a day or two of purging...there can definitely be some laughs together when you look at what you want to give away.

Recently, I finally made the effort to sell my wedding china...I had wanted to do since the divorce, but had never taken the time. It was the final thing on my post-divorce "to do" list... and finally sending off those boxes definitely gave me a feeling of accomplishment.

When you do finally clean out the clutter, it is definitely therapeutic...and it can feel like you have lifted another weight off of yourself.

Symbolism of Jewelry

There is symbolism in wearing an engagement ring and wedding ring on your left hand when you are married. As I was going through my divorce, I started to think about what I was going to do with these two pieces of jewelry that had meant so much to me. After some reflection, I actually took a somewhat unusual approach to these two symbolic pieces of jewelry.

I decided to take my diamond wedding band and save that for Grace...and I plan to give it to her at some stage in the future (she will read this book at some point, so don't want to indicate exactly when).

In terms of my engagement ring, I took it to a jewelry designer about six weeks before my ex-husband moved out of the house. I showed him the ring and said that I wanted to take the diamond and make it into a necklace...and change the look, so it was "new" in my eyes.

Also, I mentioned to the jeweler that I wanted to design a ring that I would wear on my right hand, ring finger. I requested that these pieces be ready on the day my ex-husband was moving out...as I wanted to have them to wear to symbolize a new stage in my life.

It is ironic...one does not think of enjoying their engagement ring post-divorce, but I get compliments on my necklace on a regular basis...because I wear it every day. When someone comments on my necklace, I smile and say, "It is actually my engagement ring that I repurposed post-divorce"...which usually results in a smile of acknowledgement from the individual.

I completely appreciate that I was fortunate to be able to go and work with a jewelry designer to make something I love to wear...but you can go and buy a fun piece of jewelry or repurpose a piece you might already have in your jewelry box. The point is to put something on that makes you smile and draws attention away from the wedding and engagement rings that are missing from your left finger.

Retail Therapy

It is fair to say that retail therapy was definitely a part of my post-divorce phase...both for the house...for my wardrobe... and eventually (two years post-divorce) I also bought a new car (had actually driven the same car for 15 years).

I have to admit that I have never considered myself a "shopper." However, I have found that there is something about buying things for yourself...and feeling good about these purchases...that can help as you are entering this new phase of life. I say this, but it needs to happen within reason. Now that I am five years post-divorce...I can no longer use this excuse when I decide to go on a shopping spree.

Obviously, there are a lot of women who use retail therapy... and we need to be cautious, as we can get ourselves in a financial hole fast, if we are not careful. At least for those first few months after a divorce, it can be helpful to buy things that make you smile.

Being Social

One of the things I made a conscious effort to focus on after the divorce was to schedule evening plans with friends... whether going out to a restaurant or having a girlfriend over for dinner and wine. I tried to ensure that on the nights when I did not have Grace I kept myself busy socially. Since I have been approaching my social life like this for the past five years, it is normal that I see my friends on a regular basis. This has been a great support for me in my post-divorce phase, as it has helped me stay connected to my girlfriends, and has also ensured I have filled the time that I would have been spending with Grace. It has definitely made the transition easier.

It takes some planning, but think about how you want to manage your social life in this new phase...and also recognize that there will be new experiences...like going to your first dinner party and being the only single woman there...or going to a black tie event and being the only single person at the table. These are not necessarily negative experiences I am referring to...just different experiences...and ones you need to prepare yourself for...as they can be the reality.

Social Dynamics

One major adjustment post-divorce relates to the types of social invitations I receive from friends who are still married. I am still invited to the events and large dinner parties, which were a big part of my married social life. However, now I do not get invited out to dinner with several couples. This was a major part of our social life when we were married...we were out to dinner at least one night of the weekend with other couples.

This is the biggest change that has taken place socially. I should note that I am invited to my friends' homes for dinner... either solo or with Grace and their children. However, once additional couples are included in the mix...for some reason, these types of invitations have completely stopped since my divorce. I don't take offense, as I can appreciate that it is difficult to account for the fifth or seventh wheel.

Over dinner with one of my parents' friends (who was divorced when I was young, then remarried and is now widowed), I asked her whether she had ever run into this dynamic...she said that she had also had the same experience. It was good to know I was not the only one.

Looking back, I can say that this was something that I had not mentally prepared for...and it took some getting used to post-divorce. It is something I have never mentioned to my friends...as I don't want them to be self-conscious about it... but it is a dynamic that you may want to think about as you enter into your post-divorce phase...and don't be surprised if it happens to you.

Dating Scene

There is also the question on when to start dating after your divorce...and figuring out the rules of the road relating to how you want to approach the dating scene. This is definitely a new experience...and I could probably write a separate book on the dating experiences of myself and my divorced girlfriends. We have all had a wide range of experiences, but what I have found is that we have all approached it differently. Each of us has found situations that make us happy...which is most important.

It is important to note that you should not date or be out and about during the divorce settlement negotiations, as this may affect the final outcome.

Once the divorce is final, there will be the consideration of how to introduce to your children the fact that you plan to start dating. This is one of those topics that you need to think through and address at the appropriate time with your children. The timing and approach you take to this discussion will be unique to your situation, so take into consideration how you think your children will handle this new part of your social life.

REFLECTIONS...
FIVE YEARS AFTER

The New Normal

The irony of my situation now is that I cannot imagine being married to my ex-husband at this stage in my life...the life I am leading feels completely "normal" to me...and I am very happy...so it has become my "new normal."

I cannot tell you how long it will take you to get to this point. I would say that my "new normal" took about two years to reach...and each year it gets better. Whatever you are facing, it will get better.

A friend of mine shared this quote with me after the divorce and it really resonated with me, "You don't realize the weight of what you have been carrying...until you realize the weight of its release."

The Modern Family

Society's perspectives on what makes a family have continued to evolve...due to a wide range of reasons.

I had a reality check from Grace after our first year of divorce when we were on spring break together. We were having dinner and there was a family with three children at the table next to us, whom we had met earlier in the day. Grace looked over at them and said, "They are a real family." I looked at Grace and said that families come in all different shapes and sizes, and that we were a real family, too. Grace looked at me and said, "Mommy, we can't be a real family...because a real family has a mommy and a daddy and a brother and a sister."

I realized that we probably needed to let this discussion go for the moment. When I discussed this comment with the child specialist, he said that I should not have told Grace she was wrong about her definition of a family...because that is her perspective...and only over time could she learn from her own experience that families do come in different shapes and sizes.

Family Memories...
Travel / Traditions / Special Moments

One of the points that I have focused on over the past five years with Grace has been creating our special memories together. I have reflected a lot on what I remember from my childhood, and it comes down to three key things...the travel we did as a family...the traditions we had as a family...and the special moments we had as a family.

Now that Grace and I are "a family of two"...we can still have all of those things, but just with the two of us.

We have been fortunate to take very special trips together over the past five years...just the two of us...and each trip has allowed us to create special memories together, which we will share for years to come.

There is also an opportunity after the divorce to create new traditions with your children that will allow for you to have special memories you can reflect on together. These traditions can be small moments each day, or something more significant.

From our standpoint, this has ranged from playing marathon games of Monopoly during the summer...which Grace nicknamed "Lunchopoly" because we make a "picnic" lunch, which we would eat in her playroom while we played the game on the floor.

We also started hosting a family game night with one of my girlfriends (who is also divorced) and her boys...these are some of our favorite nights of the year.

There are many special moments from my childhood that make me smile. It will be interesting to see what Grace reflects on over the years in terms of the special moments that stand out from her childhood. My hope is that she will have many special moments that we have shared...as well as special moments with her dad...as both are important. Also, when she looks back, my hope is that beyond acknowledging that her parents divorced when she was seven years old that the rest of her reflections from her childhood will be on these positive, lasting memories.

Lead by Example

As I mentioned early on, I never intended to get divorced...but when I did, I made a conscious decision to go through it in a certain way. I cannot claim to know whether it was the right or wrong way, but it was a very conscious effort, based on the points I have shared with you. I am hoping that sharing these thoughts with you will help you make what is potentially the hardest thing you will ever do...into something that you look back on post-divorce and know that you are in a better place.

One of my girlfriends, who was a child of divorce told me, "The greatest gift in my entire life that my parents gave me... was that after their divorce...they got along and never made me choose between them."

This is an essential point as you decide how you engage with your ex-husband moving forward. My hope is that someday, Grace will say the same thing about her parents' divorce.

Mother's Day Card

After five years of being divorced, I received a Mother's Day card from my ex-husband that said...

"It occurred to me as we were sitting together at our first Middle School meeting in the library that I am so fortunate that you parent the way you do, and we are almost always in complete agreement and alignment about how we raise our daughter. Thank you for being such a great mom and a dependable, steady figure in her life. Hope you enjoyed your Mother's Day."

I have to admit in reading this card...it gave me a great deal of satisfaction that we had made it through our divorce and five years later this sentiment could come from my ex-husband. It is clear to me that we did something right in our approach to divorce, and our approach to raising Grace...together.

We still have many years to co-parent Grace, but I would like to believe that we are on a positive path...to raising our very special daughter in the best way possible, given the circumstances...and that Grace can look back some day and reflect on the fact that her parents had a "good divorce."

Please pass this on

to the next mom

who needs it...

...or send her to

gooddivorce.guide

Thanks to Contributors

I want to thank the contributors to this book...my special girl-friends who have each had their own divorce journeys...and who spent hours going through this book with me...sharing their advice...guidance...comments...push-backs...and some-times reliving things we have all put in the past.

Each of them helped to make the guidance in this book as universal as possible, as each of them approached the topics covered in this book based on their own experiences.

Thank you...Stephanie Brown, Lelia Dodson, Ashley Preisinger and Judith Snyder.

Thanks to Reviewers

I also want to take a moment to thank the reviewers of this book...who took the time read the book and provide com-ments prior to publishing...Sarah Tranakos, Sharon Bauer, Sara Schmid, Lee Loughran, Kelly Rodts, Beth Ann Degitz, Kem Lee, Jeanie Bergin and Ivan Pollard.

Special thanks to my parents, Annette and Michael Madden, who have been incredibly supportive of me writing this book.

I want to thank everyone for their support throughout the process of writing this book...but more importantly, for all of the support each of them has given me over the years before and after my divorce. They have been my support network... and I am so fortunate to have each of them in my life.

Thanks to My Very Special Daughter

Grace, thank you for being supportive of sharing our experiences to help others who are on a similar journey. I feel so fortunate to be your mom...and have the opportunity to watch you learn about life and grow each year into the caring and giving person that you are to your family, friends and community. I love you...xoxo Mom

Background on the Author

Sarah Madden Armstrong was raised in Birmingham, Michigan with two younger brothers, and happily married parents (for almost fifty years and still going strong).

Sarah attended Georgetown University, as a scholarship athlete, earning a Bachelor of Science degree from the School of Business Administration with a major in Marketing. She was a four-year starter on the Georgetown University Volleyball Team.

Sarah began her career with Leo Burnett in Media. In 1997, she joined The Coca-Cola Company in Worldwide Media. Since 2006, Sarah has led the Company's global approach to Agency Management. Her work has been recognized as industry-leading around the world...resulting in Sarah being named one of *Ad Age's* "Women to Watch", and her inclusion in *Ad Age's Book of Tens* (Top Ten Who Made Their Mark in 2009).

While Sarah's work takes her around the world (she has been fortunate to travel to 50+ countries), she is involved with various non-profit organizations, including Jack & Jill Late Stage Cancer Foundation, Georgetown Alumni Admissions Program and Trinity Table Soup Kitchen.

Sarah lives in Atlanta and loves spending time with her thirteen-year old daughter, Grace...whether it is exploring a new city...listening to Grace's favorite playlist on the way to school... hitting balls at the driving range...watching a good movie... making and delivering "mudballs" during the holidays...or entertaining friends...always enjoying the special moments together.

Made in the USA
Lexington, KY
02 February 2017